II **Remember, you** ⁣**enjoy the trapping** ⁣**do a job and to up.....** **the highest** **standards in public life***II*
Tony Blair, May 1997

II **I think that most people who have** **dealt with me think that I am a pretty** **straight sort of guy – and I am***II*
Tony Blair, November 1997, *On The Record*

II **Their politics without conscience** **brought fascination to begin with,** **then admiration; next it will bring** **disillusion; finally, it will bring** **contempt***II*
William Hague, October 1997

The Big Red Book of
New Labour
Sleaze

Written by bloggers

Edited by Iain Dale
and Guido Fawkes

Hh

Harriman House Ltd
3A Penns Road
Petersfield
Hampshire
GU32 2EW

Tel. +44 (0)1730 233870, Fax +44(0)1730 233880
Email: enquiries@harriman-house.com
Website: www.harriman-house.com

First published in Great Britain in 2007 by Harriman House Ltd.
Copyright © Harriman House Ltd

The rights of the Contributors to be identified as the authors
has been asserted in accordance with the Copyright, Design
and Patents Act 1988.

ISBN: 190564132X
ISBN13: 9781905641321

British Library Cataloguing in Publication Data A CIP catalogue
record for this book can be obtained from the British Library

Printed and bound by Antony Rowe Ltd, Chippenham, Wiltshire.

Contents

New Labour Sleaze in . . . 2006   **177**

And Also. . .

Iain's Introduction

The last week of April 2006 saw the political equivalent of a 'Perfect Storm'. Patricia Hewitt was booed by nurses, Charles Clarke was in trouble over foreign prisoners who had not been deported, John Prescott had been exposed for bonking his cocktail sausage eating diary secretary and in the most bizarre twist of all, cannabis was found in the home of Defence Secretary, Dr John Reid. This followed a month of dire publicity for New Labour over cash for Peerages. Could it get worse for Tony Blair? Yes. Guido Fawkes and I announced the publication of this book.

My fellow blogger Guido Fawkes emailed me on the evening of 30th April 2006 to suggest writing this book. The idea immediately appealed but we needed to catch the wave of the rising tide of scandals that were threatening to engulf Tony Blair. So we decided to ask our friends in the world of political blogdom to help us write the book. The response was terrific and the book was printed and in the bookshops within three weeks of Guido first coming up with the idea. Phew! It's the first time a book has been written entirely by bloggers.

Of course, as soon as the first edition of this book was published it was out of date. *The Little Red Book of New Labour Sleaze* could only get bigger. And so it was that Guido Fawkes and I decided to update the book to coincide with the Great Clunking Fist taking over from his whiter than white predecessor. We felt it only natural to publish this book on 27 June 2007, Tony Blair's last day in office. It is a fitting tribute to his ten years in power.

I'd like to thank Hoby for the cartoons.

Naturally, this book will be out of date as soon as it is published but I shall keep you up to date with New Labour sleaze developments on my daily blog of political gossip, insight and humour at www.iaindale.blogspot.com

This book is deliberately inconsistent both in writing style and content. It couldn't be anything else with around 70 contributors. We hope you enjoy it.

Iain Dale
Tunbridge Wells
June 2007

Guido's Introduction

As another wave of New Labour sleaze washed up over the rotting body politic like yesterday's sewage, Tony Blair again made another attempt to make out that it was not as bad as the bad old Tory days. But it is worse I thought. At least the Tories didn't get up to hanky-panky on government premises, in government time at our expense with the taxpayer getting screwed as well as the semi-naked civil servant. Someone should really document it all so that the next time Tony claimed he was a "straight kinda guy" they would have the evidence to prove him wrong.

Intoxicated with that idea I emailed Iain Dale, knowing he had been keeping a close eye on developments and knows a thing or two about books. The next morning he replied with a publishing timetable. It was his idea to garner the British political blogosphere into co-authoring it quickly to catch the zeitgeist. This book introduces a wealth of diverse new writers to the book reading public, as for most of our blogging co-authors this is the first time they have been in print on paper as opposed to pixels on screen.

We have calculated that New Labour over nine years has produced a scandal a month on average, with little time off for good behaviour, nevertheless within these pages we document everything; shady bungs from businessmen, lying lobbyists, ministers on the make, expenses fiddled and Loans for Lordships made. So if Gordon Brown ever tries to emulate Tony Blair and stands up to say New Labour is "whiter than white", you can throw this little red book at him.

Guido Fawkes
Co. Wexford, Ireland
June 2007

New Labour Sleaze in . . .

1997

Gordon and Tony's Sleazeometer, 1997

5 sleazy episodes: Not Very Straight Guys

"Help! Police!"	30
Utterly Sleazy Guys	20
Fairly Bent Guys	10
Pretty Straight Guys	0

34 32 30 28 26 24 22 20 18 16 14 12 10 8 6 4 2 0

1997 1998 1999 2000 2001 2002 2003 2004 2005 2006 2007

WHITER THAN WH

Straight Sorta Guy
Dominic Llewellyn

In March 1997, a month before Tony Blair and Labour were elected to power, the future Prime Minister said, "We have got to be whiter than white if we are to rebuild trust in government." However, two months earlier, Labour had accepted a £1 million donation from one of the richest men in Britain, Formula One supremo Bernie Ecclestone. Labour, in both their 1992 and 1997 manifestos, had pledged to ban tobacco advertising. Once in power they published proposals to ban it from sports events from the end of 2003, with an exemption for Formula One for whom the ban would begin in 2006. The aforementioned Mr Ecclestone just so happened to be the owner of the rights to Formula One.

After much pressure Labour were forced to hand the money back with Tony Blair granting a hastily arranged interview to John Humphreys on *On the Record*, saying, "I think I'm a pretty straight sorta guy." Andrew Rawnsley of the *Observer*, writing in his book *Servants of the People*, claimed that Gordon Brown lied when telling Radio 4's *Today* he knew nothing about the donation. Brown admitted the lie privately afterwards by saying "If this gets out, I'll be destroyed". Rawnsley also stated that Blair claimed he had sought advice about the £1 million donation from Lord Neill, chairman of the Committee on Standards in Public Life, before any journalists had been in touch. According to Rawnsley, however, in fact the Prime Minister contacted Lord Neill only after reporters began to break the scandal. And his letter asked for advice about a possible second donation, not the first. William Hague, the then leader of the Conservative Party said, "No more serious allegation has been made against a sitting prime minister in modern times."

Guess who Bernie Ecclestone's lawyer was? Step forward David Mills, husband of Labour Minister Tessa Jowell and himself to become embroiled in scandal eight years later.

Although Labour returned the cash to Ecclestone, it is now alleged that Labour asked him to delay cashing the cheque to avert a cashflow crisis. It is thought that it took up to nine months for the cheque to be fully redeemed.

Fiona Jones's Election Expenses

Daniel Harvey

Controversy marred the election of Fiona Jones as Member of Parliament for Newark in 1997. Labour won the seat with a majority of 3,016 votes, but within weeks of the General Election on 1st May, an investigation was launched into how much was spent during the campaign, and whether it breached the spending limits.

The row began when Labour submitted their expenses for the election campaign. Liberal Democrat candidate Peter Harris said, "Frankly I find it hard to credit that Labour spent less than £60 a week running an office at a prime Newark town centre site during a six-week campaign. It is an astonishingly low figure."

By December 1997 officers from the Nottinghamshire Police Fraud Squad had began an investigation into the allegations, and on 12th March 1998 Fiona Jones was interviewed by the police.

Having been found guilty at the resulting court case in March 1999, she automatically lost her seat and was ordered to complete 100 hours' community service.

At the subsequent appeal on 15th April 1999 Jones had her appeal against conviction for election fraud upheld. After a High Court ruling sought by Speaker of the House of Commons Betty Boothroyd to clarify matters as a result of the successful appeal by Mrs Jones, the way was cleared for her return to the House of Commons. The Speaker told the House: "The Newark seat is not vacant."

A motion welcoming her back was signed by 34 MPs. But the damage to Fiona's reputation was done.

At the following general election in June 2001 the Conservative Party regained the seat with a majority of 4,000 and a huge swing of 7.5%.

A Choice of Diary Secretaries
Iain Dale

John Prescott wasn't the first Labour Cabinet minister to have an affair with his diary secretary. Robin Cook not only had an affair with his constituency diary secretary, he tried to procure her the same job in the Foreign Office. The only trouble was that the incumbent didn't want to shift. Anne Bullen, the then Foreign Secretary's diary secretary was a formidable woman and was not to be trifled with. But she was on a fixed-term contract which finished in June 1997. In a written answer to Parliament Robin Cook said, "Miss Anne Bullen was informed that I had decided that her fixed-term contract should not be renewed, and that she should be replaced. She was informed that Ms Gaynor Regan was being considered for the post of Diary Secretary. She was also informed when, shortly thereafter, I decided that she should not take up the position." In a separate answer he said: "Gaynor Regan had been employed as my diary secretary for four years in opposition and had worked well in the post. She was therefore an obvious candidate for the appointment, but I reached my own conclusion that, in view of our relationship, it would not be right to appoint her. I invited the Department to proceed with an internal appointment on 30 May." He never explained why he had Gaynor Regan's name withdrawn and described press reports that Miss Regan's appointment had actually been vetoed by MI5 and senior civil servants as "absolute fantasy".

The Foreign Secretary then did what most Labour politicians do in the circumstances. He attempted to trash Miss Bullen's reputation. At an EU summit he described her as "impossible to work with". Miss Bullen hit back. In a newspaper article, Miss Bullen is said to have told a friend, "It was quite wrong of the Secretary of State to ever contemplate getting rid of me so he could give his lover my job." She is also said to have dismissed a suggestion by Labour sources that she was a "card-carrying Conservative", apparently insisting, "I am not, and never have been, a member of the Tory Party." Former Foreign Office minister David Davis dismissed as "madness" the suggestion that Miss Bullen was "somehow some sort of closet Tory". He told BBC Radio 4's *World At One* programme: "I knew the lady for three years and hundreds of meetings. Never once did I hear her make a political comment of either persuasion or any persuasion."

Iain Dale's Diary, www.iaindale.blogspot.com

New Labour Sleaze in . . .

1998

Gordon and Tony's Sleazeometer, 1998

9 sleazy episodes: Quite Bent Guys

Robin Cook's Balls
Michael Dixon

The late Robin Cook will quite rightly be best remembered as the only anti-war member of the Cabinet who had the balls to resign before the Iraq war actually began. But in August 1998 his 'spherical objects' managed to get him into a completely different sort of scrape, when he succeeded in becoming the first senior New Labour figure to become embroiled in a sex scandal.

Kept secret from everyone, excluding of course the all-knowing upper echelons of the Labour Party, who had known of the issue since well before the 1997 election, Cook was conducting an affair with his diary secretary, Gaynor Regan. But on Friday 1st August 1998, as Cook was about to jet off to Colorado on holiday with his wife, Margaret, Downing Street discovered the *News Of The World* was to splash with the story the following Sunday. They had film of Cook walking out of Gaynor's flat to feed a parking meter and looking rather furtive. Small wonder, it was Gaynor's car that was parked. En route to the airport with his wife Cook received a call from Alastair Campbell. "You're in the shit", he told him. "I can buy you a few hours." Cook, knowing he had to make a decision about the future of his marriage before the story broke, decided to stay with his mistress. Sitting Margaret down in the departure lounge, he coolly informed her that the holiday was off, and he was divorcing her. Understandably, his wife was less than amused, and hoping she could be dissuaded from causing too much fuss and bringing about any serious harm to the Government's reputation, Tony Blair personally sent her a note wishing her the best. But even a visit by a reluctant Peter Mandelson to her home in Edinburgh could not hold back her fury. She alleged Cook had a history of alcohol abuse, claiming he had collapsed in a hotel room in 1987 after polishing off a bottle of brandy, and had worked his way through six mistresses during their relationship. She succeeded in fuelling stories that covered the front pages for weeks, but were no doubt rather off-putting to most of the British public, who had previously been unable to distinguish the country's latest sex god from a garden gnome. Gaynor, the lucky girl, married her troll at a Tunbridge Wells registry office later that year.

Lobbygate 1
Shaun Rolph

" I can have tea with Geoffrey Robinson, I can get into Ed Balls." It's June 1998, just over a year after New Labour's victory, and Derek Draper, former assistant to Peter Mandelson turned lobbyist, is boasting of his contacts to a potential client. But the client is really the investigative journalist and left-wing scalp-flasher Greg Palast. And he is about to get a lesson in what Draper calls, "Policy World – the little world of business people and politicians".

Draper tells how he bypassed the "useless" Margaret Beckett at the DTI and the "nobody going nowhere" Michael Meacher at Environment to bring one of his clients, Ed Wallis, the chairman of Powergen, directly to the Treasury to discuss a previously rejected merger between Powergen and East Midlands Electricity. Draper claims that now, after this meeting between Wallis and Geoffrey Robinson, that rejection "will not happen again". On 25th June, Powergen announces its intention to buy East Midlands Electricity, "subject to approval". Peter Mandelson replaces Margaret Beckett at the DTI on 27th July. One of his first acts is to approve Powergen's takeover.

Powergen were fortunate to need New Labour's help when New Labour needed them to save the coal industry by signing supply contracts. As another lobbyist, Ben

Lucas of Lawson, Lucas, Mendelsohn, told Palast, "This government likes to do deals." LLM performed the "cultural reshaping" of their clients Tesco. This included Tesco giving £12 million to the Dome in February 1998. In July 1998 a proposed car-park tax that could have cost them £20 million was scrapped.

Another partner in LLM, Jon Mendelsohn, explained how New Labour's deals with business were not just tactical but were central to its strategy. He said, "Labour's super-majority... means the only countervailing force is the media and business. So when the economy turns soft... we will make certain they stay with us. If we have business and media, the people will come along."

They certainly had the media. No government minister was affected. Geoffrey Robinson and Peter Mandelson were to be involved in other scandals before they had to resign. Ed Balls is now an MP.

Only Derek Draper lost his job. He left politics and went to California to become a psychologist. Now married to a breakfast TV presenter and with a child, he can look back philosophically on his "idiot years". "My message was quite simple really, 'I'm rich and a bit of a wanker. Who cares? You can still be that and be Labour'."

Mandelson's Mortgages and Geoffrey Robinson's Building Society

Guido Fawkes

Multi-millionaire Geoffrey Robinson's loan of £373,000 to Peter Mandelson for a Notting Hill flat was their mutual undoing. The Coventry North West MP was the Paymaster General. Secretary of State Peter Mandelson's department, the DTI, was investigating irregularities in Mr Robinson's business affairs, dating back to the late 1980s. Mandelson did not think it necessary to declare the loan, despite the obvious conflict of interest presented by an indebted minister investigating another member of the Government's affairs, when the person under investigation is also his main personal creditor. The loan itself was made in mysterious circumstances. Mandelson actually had two loans for the flat, a bank mortgage upon which he had sworn on the application that he had no other loans, as well as the additional loan from Geoffrey Robinson.

In November 1998 pressure was already growing for Robinson to resign, as evidence of more shady dealings emerged. Robinson was censured by the Committee on Standards and Privileges for failing to register the fact that Stenbell Ltd – a company he owned shares in – acquired a rights issue of 9,805,550 shares in another company, TransTec, from him. Stenbell then sold the issue to the Orion Trust, of which Mr Robinson was a discretionary beneficiary. Tony Blair gave him his full unconditional support. He resigned the next month, just a few hours after Peter Mandelson. A pattern was first established with this double resignation, in which the Prime Minister's unconditional support is the precursor to the resignation of a New Labour minister.

It subsequently emerged that Robinson had lobbied for planning permission for a massive development associated with Coventry City FC, of which he was a major shareholder through an offshore trust. TransTec called in the receivers in January 2000, a mere nine years after Robinson had taken charge of the firm (before resigning when appointed Paymaster General).

Robinson, a close ally of Gordon Brown, was never afraid to use his wealth to further his influence in the Labour Party, going as far as buying the *New Statesman*. The ailing magazine became increasingly anti-Blair under his ownership. Many speculate that under a Brown premiership, Geoffrey Robinson's loyalty will be rewarded once again.

Guido Fawkes www.order-order.com

Lobbygate 2
Guido Fawkes

Greg Palast was investigating the murky world of New Labour lobbying for the *Observer* newspaper when he met Derek Draper the former chief aide to Peter Mandelson. "Dolly" Draper claimed to have "special access" to the Treasury and Downing Street. Palast was pretending to be a potential client. Draper boasted openly of what he could do: "I can have tea with Geoffrey Robinson [the then Paymaster-General], I can get into Ed Balls [the Chancellor's then economic adviser now an MP]." All this would be available to a client paying the lobbyist's fees. Draper even boasted that he could get advance economic information. He claimed to have provided advance knowledge on government spending, information that would be crucial to government bond traders like Salomon Brothers, to whom he boasted he had leaked the data: "It's inside information... If they [Salomon Brothers] acted on it, they'd have made a fortune."

But Draper was just one of many New Labour insiders now peddling influence on an industrial scale in a way not seen since Lloyd George.

Lawson Lucas Mendelsohn (LLM) was set up by Blairite insider Neal Lawson, who advised Tony Blair on campaign strategy before the election; Ben Lucas, who conducted Blair's political briefings; and Jon Mendelsohn who handled the future Prime Minister's contacts with business. Lucas boasted to Palast that he too could get inside information about public spending: "intelligence which in market terms would be worth a lot of money". He could do better than Draper's access to Geoffrey Robinson, he could "reach anyone. We can go to Gordon Brown if we have to". His partner Lawson boasted that he could arrange lunch "in the Downing Street dining room, it's not difficult for me to take people into these people."

Was it idle boasting by fee-hungry lobbyists? No, the mentality of New Labour meant that government special advisors were often merely pausing their career before becoming lobbyists or MPs. They are integral to New Labour's influence-peddling money-go-round. Roger Liddle was Blair's European Special Advisor at the No 10 Policy Unit. A friend of Derek Draper, he described the influence-peddling money-go-round very well. He told the *Observer*'s undercover investigator "There is a Circle and Derek is part of The Circle. And anyone who says he isn't is An Enemy. Derek knows all the right people. Whenever you are ready, just tell me what you want, who you want to meet and Derek and I will make the call for you." Liddle, the PM's European Special Advisor at the time he said that, had been a lobbyist for Prima Europe. His shareholding in the firm was put in a 'blind trust' when he went to work in Downing Street. How blind he was to the interests of his clients is revealed by knowing that Derek Draper's firm bought his holding while he was still in Downing Street.

The influence of lobbyists like LLM borders on the outrageous. They rented out their contacts for clients who were encouraged to support politically sensitive projects in one area for favour in another area. Tesco got central government support for planning deregulation after it gave £12 million towards the doomed Millennium Dome as advised by LLM. LLM clients got gambling deregulated to their profit via private meetings behind closed doors arranged away from the prying eyes of the public. As with secret loans, New Labour likes its favoured lobbyists to do their dirty business in secret. Ladbrokes used LLM to lobby Tessa Jowell, the minister with responsibility for the gambling industry. It came as no surprise when it was revealed that Gideon Hoffman, the civil servant behind the controversial scheme to introduce Las Vegas-style super casinos, had secretly applied for a job with Ladbrokes' owners. Ladbrokes would only say that "Over several years, following the advent of the proposed Gambling Bill, there has been a great deal of active political lobbying between ourselves and government. It is part of the normal democratic lobbying process. We will not go into what were private meetings."

New Labour makes laws behind closed doors, drafted by lobbyists with friends in government who give each other jobs and pay each other consultancy fees. This is the sleazy world that they call "the normal democratic lobbying process".

Footnote: Derek Draper is now a professional psychologist and is married to GMTV's Kate Garraway. Rodger Liddle is head of the office of the President of the European Commission. Neal Lawson has fallen out of love with New Labour and runs Compass, a leftish think tank.

Guido Fawkes www.order-order.com

Forced out of the Closet
Michael Lyons

On 7th November 1998, the *News Of the World* rang Downing Street to inform them of allegations made by a former lover of Agriculture Minister Nick Brown. The story would be published the following day and would centre on Nick Brown's use of a male prostitute – or in tabloid parlance, a 'rent boy'.

The government was already reeling somewhat from the suicide of closeted gay Labour MP Gordon McMaster, who cited an anti-gay smear campaign conducted by rival Labour MPs in his suicide note as the cause; a claim Nick Brown himself dismissed, despite one MP being suspended over the matter. The news that the Agriculture Minister was also about to be outed had to have been met with a cry of "Not again!" in Downing Street. After all, it was barely a month after the Welsh Secretary Ron Davies was mugged by a man he was seeking to have casual sex with on Clapham Common and, as a result, quickly forced to resign in order to prevent a press frenzy before the publication of Labour's "Family Bill". Nick Brown steadfastly denied ever paying money for sex. He admitted to bestowing a number of gifts "as in any other friendship", including "small sums of money as gifts of friendship" but refuted claims that these were given in exchange for sex from his friend.

Moving quickly to pre-empt the *News Of the World*'s

scoop, Brown admitted his sexuality and, like every other Labour Minister ever involved in a scandal, immediately received the full support and confidence of Tony Blair. John Prescott was set loose on the press and denounced them as playing "judge, jury and executioner" in the outing of gay MPs. Gordon Brown applauded Nick Brown's handling of the matter on the radio, and he also was said to receive the widespread support of his colleagues at Westminster; presumably including those MPs who took part in the homophobic campaign against McMaster.

Tory Owl, http://the-tory-owl.livejournal.com/

Lord Irvine's Expensive Tastes
Alan Drew

How anyone could spend £300 on a roll of wallpaper, with a total bill of £59,000, is beyond imagination. But it didn't stop at wallpaper. Lord Irvine's official residence was restored to its original mid-19th century glory soon after his appointment. He spent £25,000 on a dining table, £16,000 on two beds and £140,000 on art. He spent £7,200 on lighting design, £56,000 for the fittings and £10,000 solely for "picture lighting". A £3,000 lavatory was installed, a further £8,000 on design and £23,000 on decorating. Just to recap – that's Twenty Three-Thousand Pounds on PAINT. Probably the strangest purchase, however, was £650 on "prototype curtain poles". In total, he presented the tax payer with a £650,000 bill. Of course, Lord Irvine justified the expenditure as essential because the apartments were part of national heritage and used for public functions.

It later emerged that Lord Irvine had made the contractors sign the Official Secrets Act and insisted upon commercial confidentiality clauses. This proved a further thorn in the side at a time when the Government were drawing up the Freedom of Information Act. The Lord Chancellor was also called upon to apologise to the DIY industry, after justifying the expensive wallpaper as quality merchandise, unlike their products which might fall apart after a year or so.

Now, the notorious wallpaper is to dignify the Westminster equivalent of a works canteen.

But this isn't the true scandal of the Lord Irvine affair.

In October 1997, he delivered a cringe-worthy speech at the Reform Club, in which he boasted of his close relationship with Blair and his position at the "cusp of government". He even compared himself to Henry VIII's Lord Chancellor, Cardinal Wolsey. Lord Irvine was safe because he was subject to a journalistic convention that precluded any media coverage. However, he, in his usual arrogant manner, decided he didn't need the protection – he handed a copy of the speech to a *Times* reporter, inviting her to quote freely from it.

In March 1998, he made a televised appearance before a Commons committee. When defending the cost of his renovation, Lord Irvine proclaimed "We are talking about quality materials, which are capable of lasting for 60 or 70 years. We are not talking about something down in a DIY store which may collapse after a year or two". He just couldn't keep his head down, could he?

In the run-up to the 2001 general election, Lord Irvine wrote personally to Labour-supporting lawyers, inviting them to a £200 fund-raising dinner. Not only did he solicit donations from barristers whose career prospects depended on his patronage, he did not even understand that there was a problem. He told Parliament "I do not believe that I have done anything wrong. Nor do I believe I have broken any current rules."

And, finally, on a number of occasions he has

attempted to sit as a Law Lord whilst being the Lord Chancellor, making him responsible for legislating and executing the law. He only withdrew when he was threatened with legal action.

The true scandal is, "the boy", as Blair was dismissively referred to by Irvine, didn't do anything about it. Perhaps Blair subconsciously felt that he owed Irvine a debt – he met his wife Cherie while they both were working in Irvine's chambers and he had borrowed money from Irvine to buy 'Myrobella', the Blair's Sedgefield home. But debt or no debt, Blair dropped Irvine from the Government in 2003 and replaced him with his other best mate, Lord Falconer.

www.dailypropaganda.co.uk

Ron's Moment of Madness
Steve Nowottny

The problem with BBC sleaze coverage is that, when it comes to sex scandals, Auntie really doesn't know where to look. It can't avoid them exactly, not when heads roll at a Cabinet level. But it prefers to blame others, and hide behind a montage of tabloid press headlines. Squirming with embarrassment, its journalists prefer to report politicians' denials of allegations they never made.

Never more was this true than in the strange case of Ron Davies, Secretary of State for Wales who in October 1998 became the first minister to resign from the New Labour Cabinet. According to the BBC account, "Mr Davies told police he was robbed at knifepoint after meeting a stranger as he strolled on Clapham Common and accepting a dinner invitation on Monday night."

Whenever a minister is under threat nowadays, of course, the press is quick to hark back to the halycon days of ministerial responsibility, and back in 1998 fresh-faced New Labour held themselves to a higher standard. But even then, being robbed at knifepoint wasn't considered a resigning offence.

The truth, unfortunately, was somewhat more tawdry. Davies, who in 1999 admitted he had been bisexual at the time, was suspected of cruising Clapham Common for gay sex.

The full story, perhaps, will never be known, but in seeking to draw a line under the incident by describing it as "a moment of madness", he was probably writing his epitaph. And while politicians of every stripe declared that a man's private life is, well, private, in reality, caught in the media's spotlight, he was forced to bow to the inevitable. Before Oaten, there was Davies.

After quitting the Cabinet, Davies left his wife, resigned as an MP and reinvented himself as a member of the Welsh Assembly. But he wasn't, so to speak, out of the woods, yet.

In March 2003 he was caught again (see page 112), in a common cruising spot known, to the delight of tabloid sub-editors everywhere, as Tog Hill. This time there were photos, and witnesses. Davies's excuse? He was "looking for badgers". A euphemism not even the BBC would buy.

Pinochet Set Free by Jack Straw
Chris Doidge

Jack Straw, as Home Secretary, put political expediency above common sense when General Augusto Pinochet was arrested in the UK in 1998. The case bounced around various courts for 16 months, based on a Spanish judge's international arrest warrant, which accused Pinochet of 94 counts of torture.

Initially, Straw entertained those who enjoyed the sight of a 90-year-old imprisoned at Her Majesty's pleasure. But nearly a year and a half after Pinochet came to the UK for medical treatment, Straw performed a spectacular U-turn and eventually let the former dictator walk free, supposedly on grounds of ill-health.External medical experts and lawyers disagreed with Straw's judgment, and accused him of wanting to get rid of his biggest headache, which was creating waves across much of the world. His judgment also contradicted the ruling made by the House of Lords, which had said he was fit for trial.

Straw's position was made complicated by the apparent legal loophole which gave the Home Secretary the role of judge and jury in the case of whether Pinochet should be sent for trial. And while Straw argued the decision would be a wholly legal one, many believed politics was at play. Straw also had to deny allegations that his student past meant he was biased against the general's regime, whom he had protested against in the 1960s. Straw was believed to be a vocal supporter of Salvador Allende, the former Chilean President who died in Pinochet's bloody coup of 1973.

Oddly, Chile itself was against the extradition of Pinochet, and on his return he wasn't sent for immediate trial. Proceedings slowly continued until May 2004 when an interview given by Pinochet to a Miami television station indicated he was easily able to stand trial.

Jack Straw, on the other hand, was later found guilty of numerous poor appearances on television and eventually imprisoned with the role of Leader of the Commons, where he would serve out his time in the political wilderness.

www.chrisdoige.co.uk

New Labour Sleaze in . . .

1999

Gordon and Tony's Sleazeometer, 1999
4 sleazy episodes: Straighter Guys, But Still Quite Wobbly

Joan Aitken
Michael Hoskin

The selection of Labour candidates for the first elections to the Scottish Parliament in 1999 raised a number of eyebrows. Many highly regarded Labour politicians were told that they were not acceptable, but the convener of the selection panel, Rosemary McKenna, managed to find space for her own daughter.

One of the successful candidates on Ms McKenna's panel was Joan Aitken, a 46-year-old solicitor, who was selected to fight the seat of Inverness East, Nairn & Lochaber. At the Westminster Parliament, this seat had been gained by Labour from the Liberals in 1997, and Labour was confident of holding it in the Scottish Parliament elections. But in the event Ms Aitken was not elected, being defeated by the SNP in what was the only seat that the nationalists managed to win that they did not already hold in Westminster.

Fortunately for the Labour Party, its dominance in the Scottish establishment ensured that a public role could be found for Ms Aitken within months of her election defeat. In November 1999, she was appointed as the chair of the Scottish Prisons Complaints Commission, where she stayed for over three years before becoming the Traffic Commissioner for Scotland. On this occasion, questions were asked in the Scottish Parliament about the role played by the Scottish Executive in her appointment

– but in typical Labour style north of the border, it was glossed over as it was evident that being rejected by the voters need not prevent a Labour Party hack from wielding considerable influence at public expense.

Mikey's Tent of Reality, http://michaelhoskin.blogspot.com/

Junket Jack
Iain Dale

We all know that Jack Cunningham likes the good things in life. And why not? After 18 years out of power who could blame him if he wanted to enjoy the trappings of power? But sometimes you can just take things to excess and that's just what Dr Jack appeared to do, when in January 1999 the *Sunday Times* published allegations of high living at the taxpayers' expense. His civil servants had leaked lurid details of his use of top-class hotels, restaurants and flights. The newspaper reported that he flew to the US on Concorde, stayed at the five-star Conrad Hotel in Brussels the previous year and ate at a two-star Michelin restaurant – all at taxpayers' expense. The newspaper report followed previous claims that Dr Cunningham decided to take private jets instead of scheduled flights to European Union meetings when he was Agriculture Minister. Sadly for Dr C, his luck soon ran out and he was dispatched to the back benches a few months later.

Iain Dale's Diary, www.iaindale.blogspot.com

It's a Hard Life
Iain Dale

You know what it's like. You've been out of power for a generation. You just want a slice of the action. And in their first two years boy did Labour ministers get a piece of the travel action. In 1999 the *Guardian*'s David Hencke reported that ministers had spent more than £11 million on ministerial travel in their first two years in power. Take John Prescott – and we do wish someone would. Mr Prescott's first trip abroad, to India, cost a whopping £99,000. We know he's a porker, but surely even he only took up one first-class seat! He followed this trip by a little scuba diving jaunt to the Maldives costing a mere £6,925. The Deputy Prime Minister followed this up with a £12,000 junket to Rio de Janeiro, Brasilia, Sao Paolo, Miami and Washington. Hencke reported that the trip "included meetings with the directors of the Cunard cruise ship company, whom he once served as a bar steward". His cheapest trip was £940 for an overnight stay in Warsaw to discuss climate change. And I always thought Polish hotels were cheap.

The cost to the taxpayer of Robin Cook's dash back to London from accompanying the Queen on a royal visit to India in 1997 to meet his then mistress, Gaynor, was £3,849. At the time, Mr Cook said he had to return to take care of urgent constituency business. Monkey business, more like.

He surpassed himself a few months later by travelling with 14 officials to the Far East in September 1997 at a cost of £169,186.

The then Culture Secretary Chris Smith also liked the high life. He seemed addicted to visiting Cannes, spending £7,000 on three separate jaunts. He also spent more than £20,000 promoting tourism and the arts in Japan and the USA.

It's a hard life being a Labour Cabinet Minister.

Iain Dale's Diary, www.iaindale.blogspot.com

The Thais That Bind

Ross Fitzgibbon

I t is a hard life being an MP, all that commuting from your constituency down to Westminster and then back every week must be a stressful lifestyle. What better way to unwind than a massage and where better to get a massage than at a massage parlour? This must have been what veteran Labour MP Joe Ashton was thinking when he innocently wandered into the 'Siam Sauna and Thai Massage Parlour' in Northampton, on eight occasions. It was during one such visit that he endured the great indignity of having his naked massage rudely interrupted by Northamptonshire Police who, no doubt to Mr Ashton's incredulity, discovered that some people were paying the Thai ladies who worked there for sex.

In March 1999 details of the raid were leaked to the press who astonishingly came to the conclusion that rather than being a simple massage parlour it was in fact a brothel, the *Mail on Sunday* then took the step of naming the MP whom had been discovered at the premises. Despite the fact that he had gained a level of recognition which had eluded him for the previous 33 years of his parliamentary career Mr Ashton reacted with fury:

"There has been intense media interest concerning reports in the Press about the Northamptonshire Police, a massage

parlour and myself. I am making this short statement to put certain facts right. The reports in the Press can only have come from one source, the Northamptonshire Police. Only they and I and my legal advisers know what happened between the police and myself."

When you think about it, it is really the police who are in the wrong rather than 'Mr Joe', as his Thai masseuse Khwanrean Maimong called him. The police compounded their wrong doing by accusing our heroic parliamentarian of giving misleading answers to their officers. Such as not mentioning that he was an MP and lying about his age.

In spite of being hailed by the press as the only man ever to go to a massage parlour for a massage Mr Ashton quit his post as a director of Sheffield Wednesday and offered to resign as an MP after the incident, but was persuaded against doing so by Labour whips who did want a potential trio of sleaze-inspired by-elections at once (fellow Labour MPs Fiona Jones and Mohammed Sarwar were being investigated for corruption at the time). This tolerant attitude towards vice seems only to extend to Labour MPs as by 2006 deputy leadership candidate Harriet Harman was demanding that the punters who partake in these services be prosecuted.

Unenlightened Commentary www.fountain.blogspot.com

New Labour Sleaze in . . .

2000

Gordon and Tony's Sleazeometer, 2000

10 sleazy episodes: Fairly Bent Guys

Gordon Brown's Maxwell 'Connection'
Tim Rowell

In 1992, Gordon Brown displayed his *prudent* credentials when he bought himself a pied-à-terre in Westminster from the administrators of AGB Research, a polling firm that had recently been forced into liquidation. He bought the flat on the corner of Marsham Street and Great Smith Street in Westminster for the apparently cheap price of £130,000.

The deal began to look suspect, however, when the *Sunday Times* reported in January 2000 that AGB Research had been part of Robert Maxwell's business empire and had entered administration following Captain Bob's death a few months earlier in November 1991. Furthermore, on the board of directors of AGB Research had been a certain Geoffrey Robinson – the Labour Paymaster General – who had not only funded Gordon Brown's office to the tune of £600,000 but had also provided the infamous home loan to Peter Mandelson.

Gordon Brown released a statement denying any "impropriety in the deal" and stating that there had been "no discussion or communication with Geoffrey Robinson MP over the flat's purchase or its financing".

The Conservative MP David Heathcoat-Amory, among others, called for an inquiry but none was forthcoming.

Gordon Brown sold the flat for £350,000 in early 2002. A prudent deal indeed.

Disgracefully Good Business
Jenny Geddes

E ven if you are a disgraced Labour hack there is enough forgiveness in the party for you to scratch some form of living... as long as the public is paying. In January 2000 Philip Chalmers, who earned £50,000-a-year as head of the Scottish Executive's strategic communications unit, was arrested by Strathclyde Police for being drunk at the wheel of his car in a red light district with a prostitute in the back seat. He did do the honourable thing and resign. You would think that thus chastised, he would start up something new in business away from the vagaries of public life. But no. Phil sees there's money to be made and his past employers see no problem in passing on business... after strict tendering rules are adhered to of course.

For it was in January 2004 that it became public that Schlumberger had hired the one-time adviser Philip Chalmers to run the Scottish Tourist Board's Visit Scotland website. The website is part of a Scottish Executive PFI contract, so just at enough arm's length to go: "Oh Phil Chalmers! I wondered what he was up to these days." But why keep a 'good' special advisor down. In August 2005 it was reported that Phil was heading a bid by French IT firm Atos Origin to secure some of the ID card contracts. We wonder how he will get on.

Prescott's Union-Owned Flat

Jenny Geddes

Deputy Prime Minister John Prescott, the token-working class member of the Cabinet, maintained his trade union links by renting a flat from one of them at well below the market rate – but he chose not to declare this benefit in the Register of Members' Interests.

Prescott was a steward in the Merchant Navy and started his political career in the National Union of Seamen (NUS) in the late 1960s. After being elected to Parliament in 1970, the NUS sponsored him as an MP and provided him with a flat in Maritime House, a block in now fashionable Clapham Old Town. The flat was provided on a statutory 'secure controlled tenancy', ie the rent is kept below the market rate.

The NUS later merged to become the National Union of Rail, Maritime and Transport Workers (the RMT), but Prescott continued to enjoy the benefit of the flat – and the benefit of the below market rent: in 2000, Prescott was paying £220 per *month* for the flat – a figure which had not changed since 1992 – while it was estimated that a similar flat on the open market would have cost nearer £220 per *week*.

In 1997, Prescott moved out of the flat and into grace-and-favour government accommodation in Admiralty Arch. But he held onto the flat and allowed his son to live there, rent free. No one seems to have asked ordinary RMT members what they thought about paying their union dues to help subsidise accommodation for Prescott's children.

Under Parliament's rules, MPs have to declare benefits given at a cost below that available to the public. When Elizabeth Filkin, the Parliamentary Commissioner for Standards, examined Prescott's case in April 2000, she said that Prescott should have registered the benefit he derived from the flat, at least from 1997, when he moved out.

Although Filkin found Prescott to be in breach of Parliament's anti-sleaze rules, her report went to the Commons Standards and Privileges Committee, which had an in-built Labour majority. They overturned Filkin's conclusion, but instead 'invited' Mr Prescott to add the flat to his entry in the Register. Despite this polite invitation, Prescott has still never declared the interest.

The final twist is that Prescott, as Secretary of State for the Environment, Transport and the Regions, passed a law (the Rent Acts (Maximum Fair Rent) Order 1999) which further limits rent increases for such properties, thereby keeping down the cost of providing his son with a free flat.

John Prescott resigned from the RMT in 2002 and gave up the flat a year later.

Speaker Betting Furore
Ross Fitzgibbon

Insider dealing in business is a criminal offence, for obvious reasons. In sport a competitor who is found to have placed bets on an event they have taken part in is usually hit with a lifetime ban. In Parliament they take a rather more relaxed view of things, as the betting scam that surrounded the elevation of Michael Martin to the role of Speaker illustrates. The office of the Speaker of the House of Commons is arguably the most important non-governmental post in Parliament – with the possible exception of Peter Hain's sun-bed maintenance man – and has the responsibilities of moderating debates and upholding the rules of the House in an impartial manner. When Betty Boothroyd stood down from the post in 2000 a new Speaker had to be chosen. Traditionally, the post alternated between the parties as a means of maintaining the neutrality of the office. As Betty Boothroyd had been a Labour MP it was expected that either a Tory or a Lib Dem would succeed her. A number of candidates were mooted including Sir Menzies Campbell and Alan Beith from the Liberal Democrats and Sir George Young and Sir Alan Haselhurst of the Conservatives. However, buoyed by the large majority from 1997 election, Labour MPs made it clear that they would not observe such a convention. Thus the ballot commenced with a record number of candidates

Candidates were voted for two at a time in a lengthy and gruelling process designed to sort the wheat from the chaff – which it did, albeit by discarding the wheat and electing the chaff. Michael Martin got the job having emerged as the man the BBC were describing as the bookies' favourite despite being a rank outsider just a few weeks earlier. It soon became apparent why. The odds from William Hill had gone from 20-1 to 8-11 as a result of several large bets – a total of more than £50,000, being placed throughout central Scotland and London.

An investigation by the Parliamentary standards watchdog, Elizabeth Filkin, found Labour MP Frank Roy had made one of the bets, but the identity of the other lucky gamblers remains a mystery. Roy felt that, "if the bookies are daft enough to offer odds like that then they deserve to lose money". He kept his job as PPS to John Reid and is currently a government whip.

Unenlightened Commentary http://fountain.blogspot.com

Smearing the WI
Chris Doidge

They jeered, they shouted and they certainly made their point. If only he'd spoken about cross stitch, post offices and crab apple jelly instead of the National Health Service!

Addressing the WI in June 2000 probably still brings Blair out in a heavy sweat after their booing and jeering forced him off the stage early during an important speech at Wembley Arena.

Beginning your speech with the words "This is the most terrifying audience I have ever seen in my life" is hardly the best way to win over an audience. And the tone of the speech continued to misfire, as Blair's words were seen by the ladies as "patronising" and full of jargon.

Recently returned from paternity leave after the birth of Leo, he was interrupted a number of times by large sections of the audience, who objected to the overtly political nature of the speech. Blair was clearly playing to the television cameras and ignoring the delicate tastes of the audience in front of him.

Some of the ladies walked out, shouting on their way, and the cameras performed a 180-degree turn. The event was a PR disaster, probably the low-point of the Alastair Campbell years.

But the real sleaze came from Number 10's feeble attempts to turn the ladies into the enemy, spectacularly failing to kill off the conventional view that the speech was a complete disaster. Rumours spread that the Labour Party had mounted a fierce attack on the ladies, digging the databases for dirt on the WI to give to left-leaning newspapers. Campbell's old employers at the *Daily Mirror* said Blair had been "set up", although even the *Guardian* admitted Blair had "bombed".

And the lecture was spun by Alastair Campbell and Co as just the speech that the WI had asked for. In desperation they tried to assert that the WI had made the original invitation to Tony Blair, although the WI had said that it was all Downing Street's idea.

Campbell played down the incident saying the WI incident showed that "a small number of people can get a disproportionate amount of attention." But the spin boomeranged when the mainstream press suggested the WI were merely the chorus leaders for a growing band of dissatisfied British voters.

http://blogs.warwick.ac.uk/cdoidge

The Millennium Dome
Martin Curtis

"If we can't make this work, we're not much of a government"
John Prescott, June 1997.

"We will say to ourselves with pride: this is our Dome, Britain's Dome, and believe me, it will be the envy of the world"
Tony Blair, April 1998

Books could be written about the spectacular and continuing failure of the Millennium Dome, but the association of Robert Bourne with the failed sell-off attempt is worthy of particular comment.

Seven months before the Dome was due to close the Government announced that the list of preferred bidders for ownership of the site after the closure had been whittled down to two bidders – Nomura, a Japanese company and Legacy, a company set up by Robert Bourne with the Dome in mind. Shortly after that Nomura was given preferred bidder status.

After a short time and not a small amount of confusion, Nomura withdrew as preferred bidders, claiming that it was not given access to the Dome's accounts. You would have thought the shareholders of the Dome would be in uproar, but, then again, Lord Falconer was the sole shareholder. In November 2000

Legacy was nominated as preferred bidder for the site. The links between Robert Bourne and the Labour Party apparently had nothing to do with this, even though Robert Bourne had donated £100,000 to the Labour Party, was a friend of then Culture Secretary Chris Smith and had donated £6,000 to Smith's constituency Labour Party. It was also pure coincidence that Peter Bourne's wife, the theatre impresario Sally Greene, had previously hosted an extravagant birthday bash for Peter Mandelson.

After less than three months Legacy lost its preferred bidder status, giving the then Liberal Democrat Dome Spokesman, Norman Baker, the perfect opportunity to use the classic line: "To lose one preferred bidder is unfortunate, to lose a second is perhaps careless."

The Millennium Dome continues as a legacy to the failure of New Labour. Visitor numbers during its year of opening were projected at 12m, but only reached 6.5m (a large proportion of whom either gained free entrance or paid a reduced entrance fee). The costs while it was open exceeded the budget by £299m. Since closing it has cost around £35,000 a month to maintain.

It would be wrong to finish without acknowledging Peter Mandelson and Lord Falconer for their vital role in the Dome project. May it be a legacy to their competence and foresight.

www.spinblog.co.uk

Byers Cooks the Books
Guido Fawkes

S tephen Byers is more recently infamous for his role in looting Railtrack shareholders (contemptuously called "grannies") but his name had already become a children's playground rhyme as far back as April 2000. Still till this day children in the playgrounds of the Midlands tease each other with the taunt "Liar, liar, you are Stephen Byers".*

Stephen Byers was Trade Secretary, Rover was, as usual, in crisis and BMW had taken over the firm but the terms were now in dispute. Byers claimed BMW had failed to adequately warn the Government about the dire situation. Byers' department released a copy of a statement from BMW's chairman, except it was different to the actual statement released by BMW in Munich. The details are lost in the mists of disputed civil service notes.

Byers was ceaseless in his efforts with regard to Rover, ceaseless in the sense that he sought to avoid any blame for the problems and ceaseless in denying he knew any of the facts that BMW had given him about the £2 million-a-day losses the Longbridge plant was suffering. Byers denied three BMW claims; that he was told that the Longbridge investment would be cancelled if a £152 million grant was blocked; that BMW had called him to warn him about the situation at Longbridge; and that he

*This is a little lie, but as with all Stephen Byers stories, a lie is to be expected.

had been told Rover was "five minutes" away from disaster. BMW was lying in all three instances he intimated.

BMW was not happy with "the ultimate lying machine". The German car giant pulled out of its investment, unable to trust the word of a government minister who would think nothing of destroying their reputation to protect his. Rover limped on for a few years before closing down with the loss of thousands of jobs.

Guido Fawkes www.order-order.com

New Labour Sleaze in . . .

2001

Gordon and Tony's Sleazeometer, 2001

11 sleazy episodes: Pretty Crooked Guys

As British as Apple Pie
Andrew Gard

In 2001–02 the steel producer LNM Holdings:

- Was owned by an Indian national, Lakshmi Mittal;
- Was registered in the Caribbean tax haven of the Netherlands Antilles;
- Employed over 100,000 people worldwide, but fewer than 100 in the UK;
- Successfully lobbied – through a US subsidiary – for tariffs on imported steel; tariffs which, according to Amicus, would be likely to cost 5,000 British jobs;
- Was the sister company of several that faced allegations of "dumping" (selling steel at unfairly low prices) by the US Department of Commerce;
- Was being sought by HM Customs & Excise for an unpaid VAT bill of £471,000;
- Was also being pursued by creditors – many of which were small British firms – over the largest corporate collapse in the history of the Irish Republic.

A company to treat with kid gloves, then?

Tony Blair didn't think so. In a letter dated 30th July 2001, he wrote in glowing terms to the Romanian premier, Adrian Nastase: "Dear Prime Minister, I am delighted by the news that you are to sign the contract for the privatisation of your biggest steel plant, Sidex, with the LNM Group. I am particularly pleased that it is a British company which is your partner."

A British company…?

Suitably reassured – the deal had been in some doubt – the Romanians signed a draft contract two days later. Details of Mr Blair's intervention – and of a contemporaneous donation of £125,000 by Mr Mittal – broke some six months on.

"The Prime Minister frequently writes to governments when British companies are competing for contracts abroad," huffed a Downing Street spokesman. "It is plainly in Britain's interests for him to do so. I do not know if he was aware of Mr Mittal's donation but it is irrelevant."

British companies…?

Even New Labour realised such a transparent fiction wasn't going to fly, and in subsequent statements LNM metamorphosed into "a British-based company"; though, save for Mr Mittal's ownership of a Hampstead mansion, it was hard to see in what way this was any more true. Pursuing the issue in and out of the Commons, opposition MPs met with the usual mix of evasion, stonewalling and, from Blair personally, haughty indignation. "It's not Watergate," he sneered across the despatch box. "It's Garbagegate."

And where there's muck there's brass; certainly for Mr Mittal whose empire has continued to grow. His donations to the Labour Party have risen too. They now (May 2006) stand at over £2 million.

Two Jabs Prescott Strikes Back
Daniel Harvey

John Prescott's time as Deputy Prime Minister will be remembered for a number of incidents. The affairs, his wife's 300-yard trip by car to the Labour Party conference, having water poured over him at the Brits in a protest about the Liverpool dockers, and the day he hit an egg-throwing protester in 2001.

As usual, his timing was perfect. It was the day that Labour had launched their manifesto for the upcoming general election and Tony Blair found himself embarrassed when confronted by the partner of a cancer patient on a visit to a hospital, angry at the treatment he had received.

Prescott had been dispatched to Rhyl in North Wales, on his 'Battlebus', the so-called Prescott Express. On his way into a hall to address an election rally, Prescott was hit on the side of the head by an egg thrown by Craig Evans, a farm worker from Denbigh.

Fortunately for the media, and indeed Tony Blair, television cameras were there to capture the egg-throwing incident and also what followed next. Prescott was seen turning round and hitting Mr Evans in the face, with a well-aimed left jab. A scuffle ensued before the two men were separated by the police and Labour Party workers.

Prescott said: "I was attacked by an individual. In the melee that followed I clearly defended myself."

Both Mr Prescott and Mr Evans were questioned by the police, but no further action was taken. When questioned at a later press conference Tony Blair shrugged off the incident, saying "John is John". Clearly.

"A Muddle, Not a Fiddle"
Anonymous

L ooking back upon it now, nearly five years after the event, nobody really remembers why the Rt Hon Henry McLeish MSP, First Minister of Scotland, felt obliged to resign in November 2001. The affair became known as 'Officegate' and related to the fact that, while a Westminster MP between 1987 and 1999, Mr McLeish had failed to net off the rent he received for sub-letting part of his constituency office in Glenrothes before claiming reimbursement from the House of Commons. The total sum involved amounted to only £36,000 over more than ten years, so it was not as if McLeish would have been able to indulge a taste for Ferraris and dinners at the Ritz. And, in any case, he was more than willing to accept the Commons Fees Office's assessment of any outstanding payments due, once the mistake had been uncovered.

No, there were three reasons that McLeish had to go. First, the Scottish media had worked themselves into a feeding frenzy over the affair, spurred on by the Scottish Tories (particularly Tory leader David McLetchie who subsequently had to fall on his own sword over the equally trivial issue of taxi fares) demanding that McLeish produce ever more irrelevant details of his expenses claims. Second, McLeish had not distinguished himself in office, having developed a reputation for the occasional gaffe. But third, and perhaps most importantly, McLeish as a Fife MP and MSP was not part of the West of Scotland Labour mafia and therefore did not command the support of his backbenches and indeed of some of his Ministers.

Looked at with hindsight, the affair is not one from which the Scottish political system and the participants in it emerge with any credit. A decent if uninspiring First Minister was forced out of office for carelessness. McLeish said at the time that it was "a muddle, not a fiddle"; in truth, it was more of a guddle.

Filkin Filleted
Chris Whiteside

Elizabeth Filkin faced systematic obstruction when investigating allegations against MPs as Parliamentary Commissioner for Standards. She became first a symbol, then a victim, of a toxic political culture in which maligning the integrity of your opponents has become a routine part of campaigning. Her treatment amounts to constructive dismissal and is a Labour Sleaze story for three reasons:

1 Obstruction of her investigations of Labour ministers, notably Keith Vaz, was inexcusable.
2 Those who made Elizabeth Filkin's position so untenable that she did not seek reappointment, including the Leader of the House, Robin Cook, the Speaker of the Commons, Michael Martin, who banned her from publishing a letter listing how her investigations had been obstructed, and former speaker Betty Boothroyd, were all elected as Labour MPs.
3 Almost worse than her removal was the manner of it. Instead of an open refusal to reappoint Elizabeth Filkin, her position was made impossible while Labour ministers claimed that the decision not to apply for reappointment had been hers. Where her predecessor, Gordon Downey, had been encouraged

to accept a second term (he declined on grounds of age), Mrs Filkin was told she would have to reapply for her job in an open competition, although neither of the criteria which would have made this necessary applied. Speaker Martin's gagging order shortly afterwards was the last straw.

Mrs Filkin was to say after leaving that a "whispering campaign" started against her within weeks of her appointment, even before she published her first report.

"Some of the briefing was so ridiculous that it was funny before" she said. "People were saying I belonged to strange political organisations. It was bizarre."

Some resentment against Filkin arose because increasing numbers of complaints were submitted to her, and she appears to have been more thorough than her predecessor in investigating them all. Certain politicians of all parties resented being investigated as a result of allegations which they believed to be unfair. Tam Dalyell, one of the few who were entirely open in their opposition to Mrs Filkin's reappointment, accused her of investigating MPs on "frivolous, trivial and false grounds".

However, the real blame for this lies with the rival MPs who made the false allegations in the first place. Other MPs across the political spectrum from Tony Benn to Peter Bottomley thought her work was "exemplary". Bottomley was convinced she was forced out for being too effective.

http://chris4copeland.blogspot.com/

Mandelson and the Hindujas
Martin Curtis

In early 1997 the Hinduja brothers expressed an interest in contributing to the Faith Zone at the Millennium Dome. At about the same time one of the brothers, Gopichand Hinduja, re-applied for a British passport (he had previously been turned down in 1990). The application was approved some eight months later.

Srichand Hinduja then applied in February 1998. In the same month the Hinduja Foundation made an offer to underwrite part of the Millennium Dome to the tune of £1 million. His passport application was refused. But the application was resubmitted in October 1998 and approved five months later. The Hindujas subsequently did sponsor the Faith Zone to the tune of £1m.

In 2001 some searching questions were asked about the events surrounding the Dome sponsorship, and the approved passport application was identified. Peter Mandelson had been responsible for the Dome as a Minister without Portfolio at the time the Hindujas' passports were approved, but by the time questions began to be asked he had resigned once and was beginning his second life in the Cabinet, this time as Secretary of State for Northern Ireland.

Peter Mandelson, of course, denied any wrong-doing and specifically denied playing a role in accelerating the application process. However, Home Office Minister

Mike O'Brien recalled a telephone conversation with him in which the Hinduja passport applications were discussed. In a rare fit of genius, Peter Mandelson later remembered but continued to deny doing anything improper. As a result of the revelation about the telephone call Peter Mandelson was forced to resign for the second time. The irony of this is that the resignation was not forced because of proof of impropriety, nor from being exposed by the media, but because Alastair Campbell was made to look a bit silly when the news relating to the Mike O'Brien conversation became known.

As has often been the case with enquiries since 1997, Peter Mandelson was cleared of impropriety by Sir Peter Hammond QC. Alastair Campbell later claimed that Mandelson's forgetfulness was due to the pressures of his role as Northern Ireland Minister.

Despite Peter Mandelson's propensity to fail, Tony Blair saw fit to appoint him as Britain's European Commissioner a short time later. Mike O'Brien's honesty in genuinely recalling a conversation that others denied is, of course, not the only reason he remains as a junior minister.

www.spinblog.co.uk

Keith Vaz's Standards

James Fletcher

Nigel Keith Anthony Standish Vaz (Keith to his friends) has been the Labour MP for Leicester East since 1987 and found his way into hot water on two occasions. In February 2000, he declared £15,000 in the Register of Member's Interests for three £5,000 donations from Mrs Lakshmi Mittal, Charles Riachny – a Lebanese businessman – and a third unnamed donor. The only problem was that Piara Singh Clair, his local treasurer, had no record of the deposit.

Standards Commissioner Elizabeth Filkin investigated 18 allegations and cleared him on all but one charge: that of being in breach of the MPs' code of conduct for his failure to disclose small donations from Sarosh Zaiwalla, a lawyer whom he recommended for an honour. She also underlined his obstruction and unwillingness to co-operate. The Prime Minister and Foreign Secretary, Robin Cook, stood by the beleaguered Minister for Europe. At Prime Minister's Questions, Conservative leader William Hague suggested Mr Blair "could keep his government's integrity or his Minister". Mr Blair kept his Minister.

In March 2001, he was implicated in the Hinduja passport scandal where both Vaz and the newly rehabilitated Peter Mandelson were accused of helping Srichand Hinduja (who donated £1m to the Millennium Dome's Faith Zone) procure a British passport.

Elizabeth Filkin investigated 11 allegations, upholding three of them. She found that Vaz made a gross attack on the "integrity and reputation" of a member of the public assisting a parliamentary inquiry and may have wasted police time.

In addition, she found him guilty of "providing misleading information" about his wife's financial relationship with the Hinduja brothers, and that he "failed in his duty of accountability by refusing to submit himself to the scrutiny appropriate to his office as a Member".

Vaz was variously censured for intimidating a witness, misleading police, obstructing a parliamentary enquiry; and his pompous demeanour turned much of the media against him. At one stage he modestly described himself as "probably the most influential Asian in Britain". The *Sun*, while backing Labour at the 2001 election, virulently sought the removal of Mr Vaz. After the 2001 election, Vaz resigned as a Minister, citing ill health.

In 2002, as a result of the second inquiry, he was suspended from the Commons for one month and lost £4,318 in pay.

He remains an MP and is currently campaigning for the banning of a video game called *Bully*.

Lord Drayson: Integrity, Integrity . . . er . . . Integrity
Guido Fawkes

You are a businessmen, you give a £50,000 donation to the Labour Party, so you get to have a business breakfast with the Prime Minister; you give a second donation of £50,000 to the Labour Party while the Government is weighing up who should be awarded a £32 million contract you are bidding on. Surprise, you get awarded the contract, you make £20 million profit on it. What value for money for the taxpayer, what a return on investment!

As fantastic as it seems, Paul Drayson gave the second donation of £50,000 to the Labour Party while the Government in 2001 was weighing up who should be awarded a £32 million contract to supply vaccines in case of a biological attack by terrorists. His company Powderject was bidding on the contract. Fortunately for him it did not go to tender. Kippers might not have been on the breakfast menu, but it was fishy enough for Powderject to get awarded the contract, making a quick £20 million profit on it. "New Labour, New War Profiteering" was the slogan.

Loaded now, Paul Drayson gave another £500,000 donation to New Labour, and was made a life peer by Mr Blair a mere six weeks later. The amazing life and times of Paul Drayson and Tony Blair has intrigued many people.

Voters might want to find out what that breakfast meeting was about. That is after all what the Freedom of Information Act is all about. Was something fishy on the menu? We the people like to see what our rulers are up to, what deals they make. After all it's our democracy. The Parliamentary Ombudswoman agrees: "I consider that very little harm would be caused by the release of the comments attributed to [Lord Drayson] and that any potential harm is outweighed by the public interest in making that information available."

The government claimed to have shredded documents that could have revealed why the now Lord Drayson received the invitation from Downing Street. The Cabinet Office said: "Any other relevant documents had been routinely weeded and destroyed in accordance with normal records management and destruction policy". That is New Labour integrity.

The ennobled Lord Drayson was appointed as a Defence Procurement minister in 2005. The appointment was defended by Tessa Jowell, the Culture Secretary, who said Lord Drayson was a distinguished industrialist (translated, "big donor"). When Drayson sold Powderject, he did so via an offshore trust to avoid any tax being paid on the capital gains, saving millions. It is not known who advised him on the legality of that transaction. It would have to be an experienced international tax lawyer.

Guido Fawkes www.oreder-order.com

Minto Street Affair

Phil Taylor

Our Scottish masters, the Scottish political types who wield undue power in Westminster, are not all-powerful. Nigel Griffiths, Labour MP for Edinburgh South, is one of the more mediocre and inept of them. He has spent most of the period since 1997 as a Parliamentary Under Secretary of State at the Department of Trade and Industry. An acknowledged Brownite, he was sacked from government in one of the early Blair-Brown power struggles in July 1998 only to be re-instated in June 2001. Another reminder, if one is needed, that this government has been wasting energy on fighting itself from the start. Besides his lacklustre ministerial career Nigel Griffiths's main claim to fame is the Minto Street Affair. Soon after his re-appointment in October 2001 it emerged that Griffiths's Minto Street offices had been used for campaigning purposes in contravention of House of Commons rules relating to expenses. At the time Griffiths got away with apologising to the Fees Office for using his constituency office during the election without their permission. Griffiths had been paying rent on these offices and reclaiming it from the Fees Office. In December 2001 the story re-ignited when Griffiths had to admit that he had owned the Minto Street premises and had not registered this fact in the Register of Members' Interests. He apologised at the time to Elizabeth Filkin, the embattled Parliamentary Commissioner for Standards. In February 2002 Griffiths was told by the Labour-dominated Commons Standards and Privileges Committee that he was wrong not to inform the Commons authorities that he owned the property which he was using at taxpayers' expense as a constituency office. Claims he submitted for office costs were "technically defective". But, predictably, the Labour dominated committee decided not to penalise Griffiths.

Note that Griffiths' ministerial progress was halted by the Blair-Brown feud but being sloppy with both the handling of money and the declaring of interests were no impediment. If Jack Straw's move to Leader of the House of Commons was seen as a demotion in the post-election reshuffle then Griffiths' move to be his deputy must be seen likewise. Nigel Griffiths continues to bump along the bottom of government.

New Labour Sleaze in . . .

2002

Gordon and Tony's Sleazeometer, 2002

7 sleazy episodes: Not At All Straight Guys

Dirty Des and the 100,000 Big Ones
Andrew Gard

"If someone is fit and proper to own one of the major newspaper groups in the country," Tony Blair told *Newsnight*'s Jeremy Paxman on 16th May 2002, "there's no reason why we shouldn't accept donations from them."

Shifting swiftly away from specifics, Blair proceeded to explain that it was really all the taxpayers' fault anyway. If only we weren't so mean as to object to state funding, there wouldn't be a problem, would there? He wouldn't have to grub around for cash the way... oh, the way Cherie and he had to grub around for a millionaire's villa each August. (The if-only-taxpayers-would-stump-up line of defence would be disinterred in the 2006 loans-for-peerages scandal.)

On this occasion, Blair had good reason to want to change the subject.

The "fit and proper" owner in question was none other than Richard Desmond, expletive-prone publisher of both the Express Group and an interesting range of other titles. One of these, *Asian Babes*, turned out not to be an academic study of childbirth on the subcontinent. Nor was a second, *Skinny & Wriggly*, a biography of Peter Mandelson. In common with *Mega Boobs*, *Horny Housewives*, *Big Ones* and 33 other top-shelf titles, they in fact constituted integral parts of Desmond's flourishing empire of erotica.

"I cannot understand why legal commercial operations, because some people don't find those activities morally acceptable, should be excluded from participating in the democratic political activities of their country," declared an unusually on-message Glenda Jackson.

Baroness Kennedy, Alice Mahon and even Tessa Jowell were rather less sanguine, but most of the sisters took Jackson's line. Some, indeed, when quizzed on the matter, seemed to be contracting lockjaw live on air.

But who exactly had decided Richard Desmond was a "fit and proper" person to own Express Newspapers in the first place?

None other than Stephen Byers, it emerged. Then Secretary of State at DTI, it was he who had waved through the takeover.

So the fact that Desmond had donated £100,000, or the newspaper supported Labour, or that the Express Group went on to appoint the Labour Party's former General Secretary, Margaret McDonagh, as the group's General Manager had nothing to do with anything, of course.

Coincidences all, insisted the spin doctors.

Cheriegate
John Angliss

Traditionally, soap opera lifestyles have been the mainstay of models and fading pop stars. That the boyfriend of the "style guru" of the wife of Prime Minister Tony Blair could attract such media attention amply demonstrates that high-ranking politicians have just become another source of debased entertainment. "Cheriegate" was an excellent example. Working from within a rich patchwork of lies, both Cherie and Peter Foster, an Australian businessman from within her inner circle, tried to mislead a British media which already had evidence of the truth. Beginning with a fairly innocuous row over the price of some Bristol flats, this protracted scandal would lead to the Blairs having to reassess who their friends were.

On 1st December 2002, the *Mail on Sunday* alleged that "convicted fraudster" Peter Foster had used the Blair name on Cherie's behalf to gain a £20,000 discount on each of two luxury flats in Bristol, which Cherie wanted to buy for her Bristol University-bound son Euan. Downing Street sent out a series of red herrings before finally claiming that Cherie would have used her lawyer if she was to ever buy flats. Two days later, email correspondence was published in the *Daily Mail* which proved that the purchase had happened with Cherie's participation. Having purchased the flats through the Blairs' blind trust, Foster had in fact helped to secure a whopping £69,000 discount.

Peter Foster had been jailed four times for his trademark violations and breaching trading standards, often by promoting weight-loss pills with faked scientific backing. He was best known in Britain for having dated Page 3 stunner Samantha Fox, but was now facing the humiliation of deportation back to his native Australia. Cherie Blair stated she had only met him once "by chance" and Tony Blair told the House empathetically that "at no point did Mrs Blair interfere in the immigration case proceedings". On 11th December, Cherie suddenly appeared at a hastily arranged press conference at The Atrium restaurant near the House of Commons and proceeded to apologise to the nation, saying that she was "not superwoman" and denying that she had "taken up Mr. Foster's case". At one point she broke down, but quickly gathered her composure.

The following day the *Scotsman* alleged that she had personally given Mr Foster legal advice on his defence case. Both his lawyer and Downing Street denied this. The *Sun*'s transcript of Peter Foster's telephone calls showed that he not only had involved Cherie in his case, but he was also trying to sell the whole story to the media. Instead, he is now using it to complete his autobiography. Tony Blair was left aghast as those "parts of the media – and it is only parts – who take these grains of truth and on top of that [build] a whole mountain of distortion and half truth" appeared to have got it right.

http://jangliss.livejournal.com

Pissed as Ken's Newts
Tim Rowell

In June 2002, the *Evening Standard* published a series of allegations about Ken Livingstone's behaviour at a 40th birthday party in London. Numerous eyewitness reports alleged that Ken had retired to a bedroom to recuperate at 11:30pm. On awaking at 1.30am Ken spotted his pregnant girlfriend (Emma Beal) smoking. A physical altercation ensued. Her friend, Robin Hedges, stepped in to protect her and a few minutes later he was found having fallen 15ft from the front steps of the house to the basement below. Ambulances and police were called to the incident. By the time they arrived, Mr Livingstone was not present.

The following day Robin Hedges released a statement through the Mayor's office. "The simple fact," said that statement, "is that I attended a 40th birthday party during which I had a fall and injured myself. It is false to suggest that anyone else was involved – it was an accident."

Two days later, Hedges retracted his earlier statement and alleged that he *had* been pressured into it. In an article in the *Evening Standard*, where he was employed as an Art Editor, he stated that Mr Livingstone had been involved and that he had been pressured into endorsing what he now maintains was an untrue statement by Ms Beal to protect Mr Livingstone.

In addition, he revealed that when he told Ms Beal he might press charges, Mr Hedges said Ms Beal told him that Mr Livingstone had said, "You may as well hold a gun to my head now."

During questioning at a special meeting called by the London Assembly Mr Livingstone said he would not be suing the *Evening Standard* for libel, or reporting it to the Press Complaints Commission because of "bad experiences in the past with such action".

Alastair Campbell Meets His Match
Jonathan Calder

The Queen Mother died on 31st March 2002 aged 101. As she personified a century of British history, and in particular the victory over Nazi Germany, any media-conscious politician would want to be involved in the pageantry marking her passing.

Certainly, Tony Blair wanted to be involved. But he met his match in General Sir Michael Willcocks – the parliamentary official Black Rod – the man in charge.

On 13th April the *Spectator* published an article by Peter Oborne alleging Blair had tried to have arrangements for the lying in state altered to reflect his importance. The *Daily Mail* and *Evening Standard* took up the story, claiming Blair wanted to be at the north door of Westminster Hall to greet the Queen when she arrived.

Downing Street, though confirming there was discussion of Blair's role, complained to the Press Complaints Commission (PCC). The PCC deliberated and decided it could not establish the facts; Downing Street withdrew the complaint. Observers saw the affair as a no-score draw.

But Oborne had not finished. Another *Spectator* article claimed Downing Street had withdrawn because it feared Black Rod's evidence. Sir Michael had produced "a long, detailed and scrupulously documented memorandum that revealed the full details of how Downing Street tried to establish a bigger role for the prime minister".

No 10 continued to exude injured innocence. Between them Alastair Campbell, Peter Mandelson and Philip Gould ("Pass the Tippex, Mandy") produced a 29-page dossier rebutting Oborne's allegations.

The dossier was holed when readers noticed five pages in the name of a private secretary at the centre of an earlier row. She had asked civil servants to provide "killer facts" for Blair to use at Prime Minister's Questions.

And it sank when the *Mail on Sunday* published the gist of Black Rod's memo. Sir Michael told the PCC he had been subject to "sustained and constant pressure" from No 10 over Blair's role at Westminster Hall. He had received more than a dozen phone calls, when the dossier admitted to only six.

Downing Street went quiet after that. Two senior Labour MPs – Tam Dalyell and Denzil Davies – called for

Campbell to be sacked, and his reputation for competence was dented.

Sir Michael's name was missing when honours were awarded to those involved in the Queen Mother's funeral, but it was clear who had won.

Liberal England, http://liberalengland.blogspot.com

Blackening Rose Addis
Julian Nicholson

"A dog... would have been treated better," was the line used by Iain Duncan Smith to describe the treatment of Rose Addis in January 2002. Addis, ninety-four, had been admitted to the Whittington Hospital on the 13th January following a fall at home, and the various claims made about her, and her treatment in the fortnight afterwards would be headline news for days.

Mrs Addis had suffered a cut to her head, and on arrival the wound was dressed, but not fully treated. Nothing scandalous there, you might think, some things just can't be treated fully immediately. The problem was, Mrs Addis' daughter, having been put off by the hospital, came to see her mother, and found her in the same bloodstained clothes she had been admitted in days before.

Mrs Addis' family went to the *Evening Standard*, which was then running a campaign about the poor state of London's hospitals, and the *Standard* broke the story; at the same time Mrs Addis' daughter had gone to see her local MP as she was unhappy at the response from the Whittington.

Of course, this doesn't make a massive scandal, and it was the response of the Government that triggered the escalation, as the Health Secretary Alan Milburn attacked the *Standard*, saying that the paper should "report facts, not fiction". This had two outcomes, first the *Evening Standard* counter-attacked, and the Addis family having failed to speak to the health secretary went, again, to Iain Duncan Smith, who then raised it at Prime Minister's Questions the next day.

In turn Tony Blair accused Iain Duncan Smith of exploiting the situation.

The most damaging aspect of the situation was to come out later, after rumours – spread by the Labour lie machine – that Mrs Addis had refused treatment because she did not wish to be treated by black or Asian nurses.

When the medical director of the Whittington, Professor James Malone-Lee was asked on *Newsnight* about the allegations that Rose Addis' refusal of help was due to racial motives he said that he could "imagine that people would deduce that". There was however, a massive fault in this attack, which was that Rose Addis was at that time being helped by two social carers from Hackney who were both from ethnic minorities.

The affair tailed out in the end as the Whittington's chief executive, Trevor Campbell-Davis, moved to apologise to the Addis family, and said that he "would not want the hospital ever to have given the impression that there was any racist overtone".

Sorry, Sorry, Sorry, Sorry, Sorry . . .
Steve Garrett

J une 2002, time to apologise a lot. To paraphrase Oscar Wilde, to issue one apology is an honest and public recognition of a wrong done to others. To issue two seems a trifle excessive. Three is definitely gilding the lily of guilt. Issuing a full five seems to be taking things to hair-shirt-and-penance overkill.

But that's the amount of apologies heaped upon Paddington crash survivor Pam Warren by an apparently guilt-ridden New Labour Department of Transport. From the originator of the email right up to the former Secretary of State, Stephen Byers, a winning hand – a five card flush of apologies will beat almost anything else won't it?

A New Labour spin man had sent the email about Ms Warren and fellow members of the Paddington Survivors Group asking nasty little questions about their political affiliations. The email questioned their motives – hinting at a political edge to the Group's demands for railway safety reform. Dan Corry, one of Stephen Byers' extra-special advisors was the writer of the email – and when the document was made public, everyone who was anyone in the Department of Transport fell over themselves to register their abject hand-wringing from 'whiter than white' HQ.

It's the usual New Labour trick – if the information goes public and it contains particularly insensitive content then consult the Department Manual, Chapter 4, Appendix 2 entitled 'How to issue a grovelling apology for virtually anything'...

Waking Hereward www.wakinghereward.blogspot.com

"A Good Day to Bury Bad News"
Tim Roll-Pickering

"It's now a very good day to get out anything we want to bury. Councillors' expenses?" On September 11th Jo Moore, special advisor to Stephen Byers, Secretary of State for Transport, Local Government and the Regions, emailed out the above, suggesting that bad news could be released whilst the media's attention was focused on the tragedy in New York. It was to spark a row that only ended in the burying of her own career and eventually Byers' as well.

In October 2001, the email was leaked to the press, causing uproar. One relative of a victim of the September 11th attacks outrage over "basically burying bad news . . . under the bodies of six and a half thousand people." Such was the intensity of the row that Moore gave a public apology on camera stating, "I would like to sincerely apologise for the offence I have caused. It was wrong to send the e-mail and I accept responsibility for doing so".

But she smirked and the image went across newspaper front pages. The next day Tony Blair called the email "horrible, wrong and stupid," but stated that "sack[ing] someone and end[ing] their career [is] too heavy a penalty," declaring he considered the matter closed.

And there the affair would have rested but for a sequel the following February. On 13th February it was reported that Martin Sixsmith, the Department's Director of

Communications, had sent an email stating: "Dear Jo, there is no way that I will allow this department to make any substantive announcements next Friday. Princess Margaret is being buried on that day. I will absolutely not allow anything else to be."

Although the actual text was misreported, the phrases stuck and reignited the whole affair. Reports that Moore was at war with civil servants left an image of a Department in chaos. That Friday Downing Street ordered the row settled. It was not just Princess Margaret who was buried that day but also Jo Moore's career.

The following year Channel 4 ran The 100 Worst Britons poll. Moore and Byers were ranked at number 59. Moore now works as a teacher in London.

Her departure may have removed her from storms at the Department of Transport, Local Government and the Regions but they would consume others until the Department was broken up at the end of May...

"We're All Fucked. I'm Fucked. You're Fucked"
Tim Roll-Pickering

It was not just Jo Moore's resignation that was announced on 15th February but also Martin Sixsmith's. It subsequently emerged that Sixsmith had not resigned after all. The row was to end in the resignation of Stephen Byers, whose name became synonymous with 'liars', as Secretary of State for Transport, Local Government and the Regions.

Sixsmith had spent most of his working life as a BBC foreign correspondent before becoming Director of Communications at the Department of Social Security in 1997. He subsequently worked in the private sector for Marconi before being appointed Director of Communications for the Department of Transport in December 2001. After the initial row about the Department's public image and the leaking of emails by civil servants, it was hoped he could restore order. However, just two months later the report of Sixsmith conflicting with Moore over releases of information reignited the whole affair.

On 15th February, Sixsmith returned from a hospital appointment to hear that both his and Moore's resignations had been announced by Byers. But Sixsmith had not resigned at all – he had been informed Moore was demanding his resignation as the price for her own departure and had merely agreed with Sir Richard Mottram, the permanent secretary that he would consider the matter after his hospital visit, with no action taken in the meantime. Mottram summed up the affair with: "We're all fucked. I'm fucked. You're fucked. The whole department's fucked. It's been the biggest cock-up ever and we're all completely fucked."

Sixsmith went public and denied his resignation, leading to a war over words as to who had said what. Byers came under immense pressure after his Commons statements were shown to be inaccurate. His Conservative shadow, Tim Collins, called it "the most clear example in human history of a man being caught out lying".

On 7th May, the Department issued a statement confirming Sixsmith had not resigned in February after all. Since Sixsmith felt it impossible to continue his job given the continuing public rows, he agreed to finish at the end of May. Two days later Byers was forced to give a statement to the House, but he refused to apologise. At the same time pressure was building on Byers after a critical report by the Labour-dominated Commons Transport Select Committee. Finally on 28th May he resigned.

Ironically, Sixsmith was still at the Department, working out his contract.

http://timrollpickering.blogspot.com

New Labour Sleaze in . . .

2003

Gordon and Tony's Sleazeometer, 2003

11 sleazy episodes: Pretty Crooked Guys . . . Again

The Ultimate Smear Test
Tim Ireland

When people want to know if that nice Mr Blair really condones torture, I begin by telling them the following true story. In August 2003 Craig Murray, the ambassador to Uzbekistan, was confronted with 18 charges, the most serious of which involved "hiring dolly birds for above the usual rate" for the visa department and granting UK visas in exchange for sex. Murray was forbidden from discussing (ie challenging) the charges under the Official Secrets Act, but that didn't stop a certain interested party from leaking those charges to the press... because shit sticks, even if the charges don't. (All but two of the most minor charges were dropped, and the Foreign Office eventually exonerated Murray of all 18 charges... but not before the smear campaign had taken a drastic toll on his health and reputation. Eventually, Murray was removed from his post for "operational" reasons.)

Compare this to the treatment of loyal soldiers David Blunkett and John Prescott... When it was proved that Blunkett was involved in an illicit affair that led to the fast-tracking of a visa for his former lover's nanny, Tony Blair described Mr Blunkett as a "decent and honourable man" who was leaving office "with no stain of impropriety against him whatsoever". When it came to light that Prescott had been dipping his cocktail sausage into staff members, Blair insisted that the ministerial code had not been broken and that it was "a personal matter".

What singled Murray out for such special treatment was his objection to the use of torture in Uzbekistan on our behalf. Murray argued that by accepting intelligence extracted under torture, we were enabling and justifying a murderous regime in exchange for intelligence that was fundamentally flawed in the first place and often spiced up after the fact. In his words, we were "selling our souls for dross".

One woman was raped (in the name of freedom, brothers) with a broken bottle in both the vagina and anus, and died after ten days of agony. An elderly man was suspended by wrist shackles from the ceiling while his children were "beaten to a pulp before his eyes". There were also numerous cases of 'suspected terrorists' being boiled alive.

In December 2005, when Jack Straw sought to "avoid getting drawn on detail" and "try to move the debate on", he made the following statement to the Select Committee on Foreign Affairs: "I have never had a piece of paper produced before me where on the rubric it says, 'We believe this has been obtained under torture'... "

Craig Murray reveals the truth behind this seemingly strong denial in a letter that the Foreign Office sought to remove from his memoirs: "I understand that the meeting decided to continue to obtain the Uzbek torture material. I understand that the principal argument deployed was that the intelligence material disguises the precise source, ie it does not ordinarily reveal the name of the individual who is tortured. Indeed this is true – the material is marked with a euphemism such as 'From detainee debriefing.' The argument runs that if the individual is not named, we cannot prove that he was tortured."

Blair's government did not launch any kind of investigation into Murray's allegations. Instead, it actually fought in the House of Lords for the right to act on intelligence obtained by torture abroad. And it fired Craig Murray for "operational" reasons.

This is why, every time I hear Blair assuring us that the perpetual war on terror is a global struggle to protect our sainted values, I don't have to imagine a boot stamping on a human face; instead, I am comforted by the image of a broken bottle in my rectum. Forever.

I apologise if you now suffer from the same condition... but that's the reality of it.

Bloggerheads www.bloggerheads.com

45 Minutes, Mr Bliar
Paul Linford

Controversy continues to rage about the 2003 Iraq War. Was it, as some still believe, a noble crusade to remove a brutal dictator who had terrorised his own people? Or was it simply the most infamous episode not just in the lifetime of the Blair government, but any British government since the Suez debacle of 1956?

Those of us who take the latter view do so largely on account of the so-called "dodgy dossier" published in September 2002, setting out the Government's case for war.

Actually, there were two dodgy dossiers. The phrase was also applied to a document published in February 2003, on the eve of the war, which turned out to have been lifted from a student's PHD thesis.

But the really dodgy dossier was the one which contained the really dodgy claim – that Saddam possessed strategic weapons of mass destruction capable of being fired at British targets within 45 minutes.

It achieved its desired result. "45 minutes from destruction" screamed the front page of the *Evening Standard*. A nation which had been in doubt about the war was hardened in its resolve. And it was all complete balls.

As the late Robin Cook said in his resignation speech, Iraq did not have any WMD in the commonly accepted sense of the words, and in publishing the 45-minute claim the Government had ignored the rather vital distinction between battlefield and strategic weapons.

A year and a half later, in October 2004, Foreign Secretary Jack Straw quietly withdrew the 45-minute claim – but by then hundreds of British lives had been lost.

Among them was Dr David Kelly, who realized the claim was wrong and attempted to correct it in conversations with journalists, setting off a chain of events that saw him become a pawn in a deadly battle of wills between Alastair Campbell and the BBC.

So was it a deliberate lie, or were Blair and Campbell just spectacularly misled? The Butler report, which found that caveats about potentially flawed intelligence had been purposely removed from the dossier, certainly suggested the former.

Either way, Blair will never be allowed to forget that he was responsible, unwittingly or not, for taking this country to war on a false prospectus.

Three years on, you could still hear the words "45 minutes Mr BLIAR" bellowed out at regular intervals by the anti-war protester Brian Haw in his long vigil outside the House of Commons.

www.paullinford.blogspot.com

Donnygate
Ed Thomas

They accepted that life through the pits was gone for good, that the future lay in a blend of entrepreneurship and Government innovation. And what entrepreneurship, what innovation – only the biggest corruption scandal in local government of all time.

Not heard of it? Oh, well, that might have something to do with the media's attitude to New Labour scandals, and the fact that this was the era of 'classic' British films like *Brassed Off*, where the big enemy was the Thatcher years. This wave of nostalgia and emotion, combined with entrenched political interests at all levels, excused anything you care to mention.

It began, as much New Labour aspiration did, during the dark period surrounding the miners strike in 1981, and ended in 2003 with at least 31 convictions for offences ranging from (at the lowest end) expense fiddling, through planning corruption, contract fraud and misuse of public money.

When challenged by the Opposition concerning local government fraud, a New Labour spokesman sneeringly told the BBC: "This latest Tory cuttings job is more of the usual desperate and inaccurate rubbish. The Tories don't seem to have checked their facts properly."

New Labour MP Kevin Hughes responded to news of

one of the arrests by saying "They'll be arresting people for taking a cup of coffee next".

According to former Labour Doncaster Councillor, playwright and whistle blower, Ron Rose, writing for Left-wing journal *Red Pepper*, "Donnygate involves the corruption of the whole democratic process".

He also notes "There has been no serious Labour Party investigation into the Doncaster scandals despite the enormous scale of the wrongdoing."

Of 31 people convicted, Rose reports that 25 were Labour councillors – and that others involved included prominent pillars of local Labour-supporting communities.

Had the 'democratic process' been truly operating, rather than being subverted by media spin-doctory and cronyism, this corruption would, and should, have cost Tony Blair dearly on a national as well as local level.

Doncaster Central has been represented in Parliament by former John Prescott "Office Director" Rosie Winterton MP since 1997. Doncaster North was represented by Kevin Hughes MP, who did not stand for re-election in 2005 and was replaced by Gordon Brown groupie Ed Miliband.

Biased BBC, www.biased-bbc.blogspot.com

The Versatile Mr Bryant
Chris Palmer

Dec700ecember 2003, and *Daily Mail* readers that Christmas, along with visitors to Gaydar profile Alfa101, found themselves staring at the last turkey in the shop... well, almost. Chris Bryant, MP for Rhondda in Wales, was quite literally exposed by the Sunday newspapers at the time, with a photograph and stories leaving little to the imagination.

The former Church of England vicar, loyal lapdog of Tony Blair, described himself in his profile as "a fit bloke, bright, solvent, single, and very versatile" although, of course, the hard time he was hoping for compared to the hard time he actually received wasn't quite what he originally had in mind. Unfortunately for Mr Bryant, pulling out by taking his photograph and profile off the website was too late, and as a result, this later climaxed with calls for his resignation.

At the time, Bob McDonald, a Labour member of Rhondda Cynon Taff Council, said: "It is difficult to believe that a supposedly intelligent man would do this. I am amazed he would be so stupid." Another anonymous councillor told the papers, "The sort of behaviour he has engaged in here is not what you expect from an MP."

Throughout December, Chris Bryant faced growing pressure to stand down over his behaviour involving both the photographs and his virtual online cruise, which included sexually explicit emails to other potential cruisers, with remarks like "I'd love to meet for a good long fuck."

According to the *Daily Mail*, several MPs were using the pants photograph as screensavers for their computers, and the *Guardian* commented "The political ramifications of using a website that treats gay sex like ordering a slice of pizza have yet to be seen" – though with the latest Mark Oaten scandal, we probably have a clearer idea.

At first Mr Bryant seemed relaxed with the situation which had thrust him into the limelight for all the wrong reasons, but the allegations had caused a certain amount of friction within his constituency. However, despite claiming he wouldn't be backing down in a hurry, Chris Bryant later issued an apology stating that his behaviour was completely unbecoming of an MP and public figure of his stature.

The former Caerphilly MP Ron Davies who was forced to resign from Westminster after his "moment of madness" on Clapham Common in 1998, due to allegations he groped a builder in the bushes at a lay-by came quickly riding to Chris Bryant's "rescue" when he claimed that he sympathised with his situation.

How touching.

www.chrispalmer.org

Tessa's Grants to Berlusconi's Film Company
Davide Simonetti

What connects Tessa Jowell with the corruption scandal engulfing her husband, David Mills, and Italy's ex-Prime Minister, Silvio Berlusconi other than mortgage shenanigans? David Mills is the lawyer behind Berlusconi's huge offshore business empire. Part of this empire is a major film company, Medusa, which received hundreds of thousands of pounds in grants from the British Government. Tessa Jowell, Minister for Culture, Media and Sport, is responsible for the UK Film Council which funded productions that were backed by Medusa. The UK Film Council, a Government-backed body which invests in British films using both lottery and taxpayer's money to the tune of £20 million a year, paid £110,000 to the British distributors of a film backed by Medusa called *Respiro*. It also invested £390,000 in a film called *Tickets*, a co-production with other British film companies. Both films flopped at the box office. Medusa also benefited from tax breaks given to Italian films made in Britain because of the 2003 UK-Italy co-distribution agreement signed by Tessa Jowell (presumably on this occasion she did know what she was signing). David Mills, who is already likely to be prosecuted for tax fraud and embezzlement regarding Mr Berlusconi's Fininvest and Mediaset companies (as well as perverting the cause of justice), has been shown by numerous documents to have played a role in Medusa. He is said to have "represented the company in negotiating contracts and commercial opportunities" since 1996 and before that was involved in the company's Dublin wing (now "de-registered") whose function was to set up tax breaks for Medusa. Not that we are suggesting there is anything wrong with this. After all, we know the government to be "whiter than white". They must be. The Prime Minister said so.

Nether World, http://nether-world.blogspot.com

Cherie's Supermarket Sweep
Martin Curtis

Cherie Blair is of course extremely highly paid. We are also aware of the financial ambition that has led to her using her status as Prime Minister's wife to make a few quid in a totally unprecedented way.

She is not averse to the odd freebie either. On a visit to Australia in 2003 she was invited to visit the world-renowned Global International store in Melbourne. When offered the opportunity to "take a few gifts" Cherie embarked on a supermarket sweep that would have left Dale Winton whooping in admiration.

Trailed by two apparently excited children, Cherie duly helped herself to a total of 68 items, ranging from alarm clocks and pyjamas through to jeans and boxer shorts. In total she is thought to have helped herself to goods totalling £2,000.

Did she pay for them? Did she leave a token donation to charity? Did she declare them to Customs? This is Cherie we are talking about.

Spin Blog, www.spinblog.co.uk

The Death of Dr David Kelly 1
Tim Montgomerie

In 1996 Dr David Christopher Kelly was made a Commander of the Order of St Michael and St George in recognition of his service of the British state. Rolf Ekeus, a chief UN weapons inspector in Iraq, nominated Dr Kelly for the Nobel Peace Price. Dr Kelly survived working in some of the most dangerous parts of the world and with some of its most dangerous weapons. He did not survive a war of wills between Alastair Campbell's Downing Street spin operation and the BBC, however.

Dr Kelly's job description included a media liaison role and over years of overseeing weapons decommissioning he had built up many contacts. He used one of these contacts, Andrew Gilligan, to publicise his objections to the Government's infamous claim that Saddam Hussein could launch deadly battlefield weapons in 45 minutes. On the back of his meeting with Dr Kelly, Gilligan famously reported on the BBC *Today* programme on 29th May 2003 that Downing Street had "sexed up" the Iraq War intelligence dossier and that Alastair Campbell was the guilty man.

Alastair Campbell had been a bully throughout his time as Blair's spinmeister. Often referred to as the "real deputy Prime Minister" he enjoyed more influence on the Blair project than almost every cabinet minister. Campbell's fingerprints were all over Blairism's worst features. The briefing against opponents. The obsession with tomorrow's headlines. The distortion of statistics. The defence of the indefensible.

Campbell turned his whole PR operation against the BBC after Gilligan had made his incendiary allegations and, with a lot of help from Lord Hutton, he eventually succeeded in removing the BBC's top brass.

In the middle of this war David Kelly committed suicide although many conspiracy theorists, relying on expert testimonies, still believe that he did not end his own life. Dr Kelly was found dead near his Oxfordshire home – eight days after the Ministry of Defence had confirmed his identity to a hungry pack of journalists. The Whitehall machine exposed this private, retiring man to the hottest of media frenzies. The Hutton Report was widely seen as a whitewash but even Lord Hutton concluded that the Ministry of Defence had failed to properly protect one of its key employees.

Alastair Campbell left Downing Street in August 2003 after the press and public had become sick of his media manipulation. His departure was spun as the end of the era of spin but the spinner returned to Blair's side for the 2005 general election. His return cost Labour donors £47,000.

Editor, Conservative Home, www.conservativehome.com

The Death of Dr David Kelly 2
Richard Bailey

On 24 Sept 2002, the Government published an intelligence dossier containing the now legendary claim that the Iraqis could "deploy these weapons [of mass destruction] within 45 minutes of the decision to do so." On 29th May 2003, after the Iraq war, the BBC broadcast an unscripted live report by Andrew Gilligan on the Radio 4 *Today* programme, stating that "one of the senior officials in charge of drawing up the dossier says that the Government knew the 45 minute claim was wrong and a week before publication, Downing Street ordered it to be sexed up…" On 30 June 2003, after weeks of controversy, Dr David Kelly admitted to his boss that he had met Andrew Gilligan in an unauthorised meeting a week prior to the fateful BBC report.

To qualify for this book, an event must carry an element of sleaze rather than simply scandal. It is an unfathomable scandal that our Government might consider leading our country into war on a false or exaggerated prospect, but it is sleazy beyond belief for our Government machine, empowered by Tony Blair and his inner circle of advisors and loyal Ministers, to conspire to name and smear a top civil servant in a bid to save their own necks and hide the truth.

The pressure on the Government, on Blair, Campbell and Hoon was immense and increasing. On 8th July, the

Ministry of Defence issued a press release stating that an individual official had come forward. Suddenly, an eminent government scientist had become a pawn in a vicious game between the Government and the BBC, with both attempting to force the other into revealing the name of the source and thus defend their own version of events. A supporting brief for MOD press officers contained the advice that if the right name is suggested by the media, they could confirm it. By 6pm the following day, Dr Kelly's name had become public.

In the final week of Dr Kelly's life, the Government's primary concern was the limitation of damage that might come from Dr Kelly's appearance before the FAC and Intelligence Select Committee and the complete demolition of Andrew Gilligan's reputation. As Campbell said in his diary entry for 4th July 2003 "GH (Geoff Hoon) wanted to throw the book at him [Kelly] but there was a case for getting a plea bargain. GH and I agreed that it would fuck Gilligan if that [Kelly] was his source."

Dr Kelly was cut loose by the MOD and left to cope with the pressure of media attention without any of the support afforded to Ministers and other public figures. It remains the Government's position that neither Geoff Hoon nor Tony Blair had any involvement in the media handling strategy that allowed Kelly's name to be confirmed to media should they suggest it first. It is stated that the Director of Communications at the MOD, Ms Pam Teare, devised the strategy herself without reference to or clearance by ministers.

I can only assure you that, as a former Whitehall press officer myself, there was no occasion on which any statement was given nor Question and Answer brief written without explicit and full clearance by the minister in whose name it would be released. I can also assure you that, as the press officer responsible for the Hutton Inquiry media arrangements, all the lines prepared for the event were cleared by senior officials at Number 10 Downing Street.

On 17th July 2003 Dr David Kelly walked from his house and committed suicide in the tranquil Oxfordshire countryside and plunged Tony Blair and his Government into the Hutton Inquiry and months of unremitting exposure. In his closing address, counsel for the Kelly family said that one of the aims of the Kelly family in the Inquiry was that the "duplicity of the Government in their handling of Dr Kelly should be exposed". The dishonourable, underhand and frankly incompetent way in which the MOD and Number 10 Downing Street handled Dr Kelly immediately prior to his death was revealed in all its glory, but no knock-out blow was ever landed in evidence to the Hutton Inquiry and the Government wriggled free, released by the Hutton report which was, ironically for New Labour, condemned as an Establishment whitewash.

Richard Bailey was press officer to the Hutton Inquiry, www.baileyblogspot.blogspot.com

Badger Watching
George Street

March 2003 – Ron Davies, the former Welsh Secretary, announced he would be leaving politics following newspaper claims that he took part in a gay sex act with a stranger in a public beauty spot at Tog Hill, just off the M4 north of Bath in Somerset. Davies claimed that initial denials that he had been in the area at all had been based on confusion: "I have actually been there when I have been watching badgers". For some reason, local papers were unable to publish the following "Country Diary" piece at the time of the Tog Hill incident. The short reflection on rural life and customs can now be reproduced in full for the first time.

A Country Diary: Tog Hill, Somerset – by Cedric Gravel:
To Tog Hill, the early spring morning sunlight dappling softly on the hidden telephoto lenses of that most shy of creatures, Sun *photographers, as they conceal themselves in the lower bushes. As I sit and watch, I see one slowly emerging: small head, thick short neck, beady little eyes and long wedge-shaped body, yes, the European badger (meles meles) snuffles gently in the undergrowth unconcerned and unaware of the part-time plasterer from Bristol seeking a bit of rough trade in the mosses and undergrowth of this most attractive lay-by. Approaching now from the deeper undergrowth, small head,*

short thick neck and that familiar wedge-shaped body – it's our old friend, the Labour member for Caerphilly in the Welsh Assembly. The outcome of these couplings is predictable. Initial denial, claims of devastation and bruising and finally attaching all blame to the media. Other denizens of this wooded paradise will eulogise about the tragic end of a political career while the third wife will wonder what the hell she's let herself in for. At some point the swines from the local constabularly will be involved, names in paper, etc. Nature red in tooth and claw, the vicious cycle of life in the under-growth . . . I remember when Bertie and myself did our trip to the Ardennes just before the War, we (that's enough this week, Cedric. – Editor).

As Far fetched As . . . http://bucket-of-shit-from-china.blogspot.com

Not an Extremely Disturbed Person
Steve Garrett

In November 2003, Children's Minister Margaret Hodge was forced to eat upwards of twenty grands' worth of very public humble pie. Ten thousand went to a charity, the other half paid for Mr Demetrius Panton's court costs. The reason she swallowed this sticky, indigestible Hodge-podge of stodge was just payment for an utterly contemptible attempt to discredit an honest and honourable man. In a letter to BBC Chairman Gavyn Davies, she'd accused Mr Panton of being "an extremely disturbed person" Hodge has always been a bit intemperate, a bit gung-ho and a tad hasty with her use of language – but this episode really plumbed the depths. Mr Panton said, "I have experienced the personality politics of the gutter. I personally think that's not the kind of politics that we expect from the Minister of State for children." She sent the letter in an apparent attempt to stop the BBC from investigating Panton's claims of child abuse whilst he lived in Islington's care homes during the 1980s. Hodge was head of Islington Council at the time. The BBC programme would obviously have embarrassed Hodge, testy questions may have been asked about her involvement – especially as she had rather ironically and incomprehensibly been promoted to "Minister for Children" in Blair's whiter than white government. Typically, as with all New Labour ministers, Hodge refused to resign. Typically, as with all New Labour ministers, she received "full and unequivocal" backing from Tony Blair. Hodge's letter of apology was abject, grovelling and total in a desperate attempt to bring the matter to a close. Fortunately, Mr Panton is made of sterner stuff, he insisted on a charity donation, court costs and a very public apology to him. I wonder if Mr Panton has ever thought of running for Parliament?

Footnote: Tony Blair promoted Margaret Hodge in his May 2006 reshuffle.

Waking Hereward www.wakinghereward.blogspot.com

Fancy a Brazilian?
Chris Palmer

They say it's hot inside Brazil – and Clive Betts should know. In July 2003 he was suspended from the House of Commons for his part in a bogus immigration application by his Brazilian former male escort and lover – the same rent boy that he employed as his parliamentary assistant.

Caught out by the notorious *Sun* newspaper as a closet gay while holidaying in Venice with said rent boy, whom he loaned (yes, another one of these mystical Labour loans that never seem to need repaying) over £4,000 to apparently help with his "tuition fees" – the papers claimed that by applying for a security pass allowing the "former" escort to wander unescorted in Westminster, he was seriously undermining Parliament and breaching the MPs' Code of Conduct.

The Commons Standards and Privileges Committee agreed and found the MP for Sheffield Attercliffe had acted "extremely foolishly" in agreeing to photocopy a doctored document which his lover had hoped would help him extend his stay in the UK (which, guess what, it did) and attempting to gain a security pass easily misused in the wrong hands.

However, in Clive's own little world this was only "an error of judgement". How many times have we heard that from Labour before and since?

In the event Clive Betts apologised to Parliament, claiming that because he effectively owned up (notably after being caught) and asked the Complaints Committee to investigate his disgraceful conduct, that made it OK... Well that make's everything all right then – obviously.

Political Crosswords www.chrispalmer.org

New Labour Sleaze in . . .

2004

Gordon and Tony's Sleazeometer, 2004

11 sleazy episodes: Still Pretty Crooked Guys

- "Help! Police!" (30)
- Utterly Sleazy Guys (20)
- Fairly Bent Guys (10)
- Pretty Straight Guys (0)

Axis values: 34, 32, 30, 28, 26, 24, 22, 20, 18, 16, 14, 12, 10, 8, 6, 4, 2, 0

Years: 1997, 1998, 1999, 2000, 2001, 2002, 2003, 2004, 2005, 2006, 2007

The Resignation of Beverley Hughes
George Surgenor

The resignation of Beverley Hughes as Immigration Minister in April 2004 was shameful in many ways. Not only did she preside over a system that allowed thousands of bogus immigrants into Britain, she misled the public and then blamed her civil servants for her failings.

Hughes had been warned for more than a year that bogus immigrants from Eastern Europe were being waived through by the Home Office. Junior minister Bob Ainsworth had sent her a two-page memo warning that staff had been "demoralised" at the "weakening of the immigration control". She had acknowledged this, though in her reply seemed to be more concerned with the entitlements of offenders and refused to inform the Bulgarian authorities of suspected bogus applicants, because it "raised human rights issues".

Her failure to act on these warnings prompted two civil servants to go public with the scandal. James Cameron, the British consul in Romania, claimed that "suitcase loads" of false applications had been waived through by the Home Office, despite earlier warnings. Cameron was recalled from Bucharest and given a final warning on his conduct. Steve Moxon tried to inform Hughes of fast-tracking in Sheffield, but his e-mails were ignored and he was refused a meeting. After initially denying such a policy, Hughes was forced to admit she had authorised such a policy, and then blamed it on the "excessive zeal of officials". Hughes blamed a secretary for not passing on Moxon's email and refused to apologise to him. Moxon was fired for "embarrassing ministers".

Hughes then misled the public, by announcing on *Newsnight* that she had not been informed of such abuse even though she had sent two letters of reply to Ainsworth. She announced that she was "neither incompetent nor dishonest", despite the fact that there was firm evidence of one and considerable suspicion of the other. Hughes previously ignored warnings before the death of the Chinese cockle pickers on Morecambe Bay. She also condemned a Channel Four television programme as "unspeakably sick", before admitting that she had in fact not seen it. In spite of this, Blunkett saluted her "integrity" and said she had been an "effective minister". Cameron and Moxon were punished for exposing the scandal, Blunkett and Hughes were recalled to the Government after causing it. After the scandal, Prime Minister Blair promised to take "a close interest" in immigration matters, which no doubt explains the current shambles.

Vote Early, Vote Often
Michael Moncrieff

The desperation of the Labour Party reached a new low when Election Commissioner Robert Mawrey QC upheld allegations made by opposition parties that six Labour councillors had engaged in electoral fraud during the 2004 Birmingham Council elections.

Opposition supporters lodged petitions amid concerns over vote rigging and intimidation during the election, all of which were hotly denied by the Labour councillors involved. However, three of those being investigated had been found by police handling unsealed postal ballots in a deserted city warehouse. This 'vote-rigging' factory, was more successful than the other infamous Birmingham factory at the time (the Rover plant which Labour shamelessly threw money at in 2005 to secure votes) as the judge ruled that at least 1,500 votes had been fraudulently cast in a massive, organised scam. Judge Mawrey also declared that the elections to the wards of Aston and Bordesley Green, where all six were elected, were null and void, and ordered new ones in which they were not allowed to stand.

Since then, one of the men stripped of his council seat, Muhammed Afzal, has been cleared of all charges. The ruling on the others remains, that they collected postal votes for the election through forgery and deception.

Both before and after the scandal, enquiries had high-lighted how open the postal ballot system was to abuse. At the 2005 general election, John Humphrys was denied the right to vote over a postal ballot mix-up. Since then, concerns have been raised in London, Stoke and again Birmingham about the possiblity of postal vote fraud. The government claims to have tightened up the system, but the stench of sleaze still hangs heavy over the Labour Party following their fraudulent behaviour in Birmingham's 2004 election.

Surely there is nothing so sleazy as having to rig an election to ensure victory?

Paying for it
James Cleverly

She was one of the 101 female MPs who were swept into office on the crest of the 1997 New Labour wave. They were dubbed "Blair's Babes" and the implied criticism was that they were just window dressing, only there only to make the Labour Party look good. Indeed many of these female MPs were surprise additions to the Labour benches having stood in seats which no one at the time expected to turn from blue to red. Oona King was never someone who could be described as window dressing. With a first class degree in politics and years of experience in the European Parliament she was clearly one to watch. And watched she was. It seems that despite her intelligence, qualifications and experience at least one Labour MEP saw her basically as a "shag". She is, after all, very attractive. Sir Robert Walpole once said that "Every man has his price" and this particular MEP was keen to find out if Oona had one too. But how much to offer? Too little could result in a refusal, too much would get the desired result but would leave the nagging feeling that you could have got a better deal. Our randy Labour MEP came up with the ideal solution, offer a huge amount of someone else's money. The figure was £10,000 and the money was yours. Now as I have said (too often if my wife is to be believed), Oona King is an attractive woman, but £10,000 is a lot of money. A lot of your tax money. Oona told him to "go to hell". Supermodel Linda Evangelista once declared that she wouldn't "get out of bed for less than $10,000 a day". It seems that our Oona won't get into bed for £10,000. And who could blame her?

So what have we learned from this little episode? That there were some randy Labour politicians who thought nothing of propositioning their subordinates? That there were some people in the Labour Party who thought nothing of spending thousands of pounds of public money for their own gratification? Unfortunately yes to both, but at least those days are behind them. (Shurely shome mishtake – Ed)

www.jamescleverly.blogspot.com

What They Did on Their Holidays
Anonymous

It is often said that Scotland is a village. It was no surprise, therefore, to learn that Scotland's First Minister, Jack McConnell, and his family were friends with Scotland's first lady of broadcasting, Kirsty Wark, and her family. But eyebrows were raised when it became known that the McConnells had spent the New Year holiday at the end of 2004 with the Warks in the latter's Majorcan villa. The bold Jack saw nothing wrong in such an arrangement; indeed he did not even feel obliged to record it in the Scottish Parliament's Register of Members' Interests.

It seems not to have occurred to either Jack or Kirsty that their shared holiday might compromise their respective positions in the political and broadcasting worlds. And, for reasons which mystified most observers, the parliamentary standards commissioner deemed that the First Minister did not need to have declared the holiday. Wark, on the other hand, was apparently put on probation by the BBC and she was allegedly dropped from presenting the Scottish coverage of election night.

There are two lasting memories of the affair. The first involves the unanswerable question of why on earth would an obviously bright and successful media star want to spend a holiday with a hack politician like McConnell? The second involves further confirmation of

McConnell's execrable taste in clothes. After his earlier fashion faux pas in wearing a pinstripe kilt in New York and thus embarrassing the entire Scottish nation, on this occasion he allowed himself to be photographed wearing beige shorts, white socks and trainers. As the First Minister is not exactly blessed with the physique of a racing snake, it was something of a mercy that the pictures were confined to the Scottish press.

Lord Fire Starter

Bel Andrew

L ord Watson of Invergowrie was the Labour MSP for Glasgow Cathcart until he was sent to prison in September 2005 for setting fire to a hotel. He had previously been a Labour MP from 1989 to 1997.

It all began in November 2004, at the Scottish Politician of the Year Awards. The function was held at the Prestonfield House Hotel in Edinburgh. There was a private VIP function following the awards, to which the noble lord was invited. Drinks flowed throughout the evening, and Lord Watson took full advantage of the free bar.

The party ended, and the guests departed, but Lord Watson was not yet ready to leave. He stayed behind, aggressively demanding more drink as the staff tried to clear up. He refused to accept that the bar was closed, and frustrated staff ended up giving him a bottle of wine to get him off their backs. Fed up with his boorish behaviour, the organiser of the event was eventually forced to remonstrate with him. Lord Watson was not happy. He waited until everyone had gone, and then crept into the reception room. Crouching in the still night, he fished out some matches from his sporran and set the curtains alight. The fire caused about £4,500 worth of damage. Unfortunately for him, his every move was captured on the hotel's CCTV. Imagine his shock when

the Police came calling. At first, he denied any involvement, but later changed his mind. He pleaded guilt to
wilful fire raising, and was jailed for 16 months.

Bel is Thinking, www.beltoday.com

Cherie Blair and The Goldfish Bowl
Tim Rowell

In 2004, Cherie Blair and the popular social historian Cate Haste (author of *Nazi Women* and Melvyn Bragg's wife) wrote a book entitled *The Gold Fish Bowl: Married to the Prime Minister*. On the face of it, it was an interesting, if rather pedestrian study of the contrasting experiences of the spouses of British Prime Ministers – from Clarissa Eden through to Cherie Blair and including the only male to occupy the role, Denis Thatcher.

LIFE INSIDE THE GOLDFISH BOWL.

What followed, however, began to mire the book, its co-author and the co-author's spouse in controversy. Cherie Blair embarked upon a 'world tour' to promote the book from Hay-on-Wye to Washington DC, and from Auckland to Florida. Invariably billed as "An Afternoon with Cherie Booth", Cherie was earning somewhere in the region of £750 per minute to give a short speech and answer questions about her life in Number 10 and her experiences of being married to the Prime Minister. In total, Cherie is believed to have earned in excess of £500,000 from her speaking tours.

Norma Major may have penned a book exploring the history of Chequers but never embarked on such brazen exploitation of her position.

The Blairs are believed to have a mortgage debt of almost £4million on their properties in London, Bristol and Sedgefield. Cherie earned roughly £30,000 per talk – that's roughly two months' mortgage payments. A very nice little earner.

The Lies Over Abu Ghraib
Robert Halfon

The Abu Ghraib debacle has been one of the most difficult episodes of the Iraq war – greatly undermining the justified humanitarian reasons for invading Iraq. It presented a propaganda gift to those opposed to the war. Yet instead of acknowledging the problem and the human tragedy that had occurred, Tony Blair pretended that his Government knew nothing about it.

On 12th May 2004, Tony Blair denied in the House of Commons that he or any other Minister had been informed about the allegations of the abuse of prisoners in Abu Ghraib. Yet this was far from the truth. It subsequently emerged that the then Foreign Minister Bill Rammell had been informed almost two months earlier.

On 18th March 2004 Mr Rammell had been given information about the alleged abuse by the President of the International Committee of the Red Cross (ICRC). On 19th March, the Foreign Office was given a report about the abuses by the ICRC.

It beggars belief that Mr Blair, or the Foreign Secretary Jack Straw, was not told about about the ICRC Report, unless Mr Rammell failed to tell the Foreign Secretary. In fact, on 11th May Jack Straw said that he should have been given a copy of the report.

Even giving Tony Blair the benefit of the doubt, why did he never correct the public record or apologise for having misled Parliament? Why did his Foreign Minister fail to pass the information to Downing Street? Why did he not make any inquiries to check whether or not his Ministers had been informed about the alleged abuses? Why was Mr Blair content, either not to check the facts or content to give out false information on a matter as serious as Abu Ghraib?

Two Fingers to Regionalisation
James Frayne

The massive 'No' vote in the North East referendum on whether there should be an elected Regional Assembly in November 2004 was a complete shock to the Government. It was never meant to happen. From the very beginning the Government had done all it could to make sure it was a walk in the park and its campaigns showed their willingness to do anything to try to secure victory.

For a start, the Government loaded the referendum question in favour of a yes vote by making sure the ballot paper included a preamble which claimed the new Assembly would take considerable powers from central Government, including "regional economic development". This should never have been there given that this was the biggest single issue of contention in the referendum – we argued that the Assembly would have no real power over things like economic development and that the Assembly was a White Elephant. Such a preamble was like having a "Vote Yes" sticker stuck on the ballot paper.

The Government also insisted that the referendum be an all-postal vote election despite concerns that all-postal votes were more open to fraud. This is obviously true but the advantage the Government had in an all-postal vote was that the various Yes campaigns (Yes 4 The North East, the Labour Party, the unions etc) had a much bigger and better campaigning infrastructure to make sure that postal votes could be collected and turnout raised. Many hoped that this minimised the chances of a shock result in the context of a low turnout and a small but motivated No Campaign.

So the Government made sure it started with huge built-in advantages and they continued to behave without respect for the rules. Above all Government politicians blurred the line between campaigning as Labour politicians – which was acceptable – and Government officials – which was not. This all came to a head when John Prescott briefed a front-page splash in a friendly newspaper saying that he had spoken to others in the Government and had managed to get a guarantee that they would secure more power over transport for the region after a yes vote. This was an obvious breach of the rules but the weakness of the Electoral Commission meant that nothing could be done and, as the Government knew all too well, there was nothing in it for the No Campaign to whinge about the technicalities of electoral rules when we wanted to be smashing the Government over the head on other issues.

This sort of political activity was not limited to national politicians. One local council used taxpayers' money to print 40,000 stickers to go on wheelie-bins backing a local government reorganisation that was dependent on a yes vote. This broke the rules about government bodies advertising during the election campaign and the Electoral Commission forced the council to remove the stickers later.

But councils were able to get their own back. Whilst it generally takes an eternity for council workers to get round to doing anything quickly, they were extremely efficient at forcing No Campaign supporters to remove posters and roadside banners which apparently breached some regulation or another. Council workers even went on to private land to try to remove "Politicians talk, we pay" posters. Some banners were literally removed within hours. It often felt like campaigning in Soviet Russia.

And all of this was taking place within the context of an unbelievably unpleasant campaign from New Labour's top politicians and their campaigners. As the polls began to move from yes to no, the accusations and personal attacks increased and became more vitriolic. This included the accusation that the No Campaign were "all Tories", and "Rather Arrogant Toff Southerners" ("RATS" – yes, really). It included claims that the No Campaign's businesspeople didn't have the interests of the region at heart and towards the end it predictably included the pathetic argument that the No Campaign was on the same side as the BNP, who also wanted a No vote.

The final result was staggering – the people of the North East voted by nearly 4-1 against a Regional Assembly (78-22 per cent). But the campaign was more brutal and unpleasant that most people realise. It revealed the very worst traits of this Government's senior politicians – their disregard for the public, their win-at-all-costs mentality, and their willingness to intimidate. The No vote should have marked a turning point in

British politics where politicians were forced to change their behaviour. Unfortunately, it has been politics as usual ever since and it shows no signs of changing.

www.taxpayersalliance.com

Creative Accounting
Damon Lambert

The year 2001 saw the introduction of the government's Political Parties, Elections and Referendums Act. One of the conditions is that every quarter each political party has 30 days to submit a return of all the donations it received in the previous three months, rather similar to what thousands of businesses regularly do when submitting details of sales in their VAT returns.

Could Labour comply with its own simple requirement? As early as the third quarter of 2002, the Electoral Commission held meetings with Labour to discuss its non-compliance. In one quarter Labour forgot a whopping £1.8 million of donations. In late 2003 Labour got investigated but no further action was taken because "the Commission is satisfied that the Party Treasurer took all reasonable steps and exercised due diligence". The Party Treasurer, Jack Dromey, was so reasonable and diligent he never questioned how £17.9 million of general election costs got funded, and hence did not twig the existence of £14 million of loans from individuals. Labour's excuse that it was having transitional problems adopting to the new regime does not whitewash – the task of recording every donation and sending the list to the Electoral Commission could be done by any trainee accountant. Did Labour learn? Since the Electoral Commission's investigations, Labour has reported late donations in seven out of eight quarters, making it possibly the only examination whose pass rate has dropped in recent years. Curiously, most other parties have declared impermissible donations, and returned the sums to the would-be donors. In four years, Labour, by far the biggest recipient of largesse, has never declared a single 'bad' donation.

Taxcutter, http://.thetaxcutter.blogspot.com

Marxist Milibands?
Iain Dale

We all know that New Labour doesn't really approve of offshore trusts and tax loopholes. Well, that's their public position anyhow. The Chancellor of the Exchequer has been assiduous in closing inheritance loopholes, ably assisted over the last nine years by his policy assistant Ed Miliband (brother of Cabinet Minister David), now a Labour MP. Ed's and David's father Ralph Miliband, the Marxist historian and uber-Leftie died in 1994 having transferred almost all his assets, including homes in London and Oxfordshire, to his wife. Strangely, the family posthumously rewrote his will to give the two MP brothers a 20 per cent share of the family home in London, having been advised to do so by tax accountants. David first declared a "20% share of family home in London" on the MPs' Register of Interests in 2002, although it has curiously disappeared from the latest version. Ed Miliband has never registered it. The *Sunday Times* reported:

"This scheme is called a "deed of variation" and was high-lighted by the chancellor in opposition as an unacceptable way in which the wealthy avoid paying death duties. It allows people to inherit assets tax-free even if this goes against the wishes of the deceased. Had Ralph Miliband's will not been altered, David and Ed would have inherited the house (or the

money raised from its sale) when their mother Marion died and would have faced a tax bill equivalent to 40% of its value. Instead they were able to cash in on their stakes when the family's four-bedroom townhouse in Primrose Hill, north London, was sold earlier in the summer. When it was sold they may have paid other taxes. The Milibands claim that the scheme was not established to reduce tax. However, leading accountants believe that such schemes always reduce inheritance tax bills. John Whiting, head of tax at Price Waterhouse Coopers, the accountancy firm, said: "The reason people use deeds of variation is to save inheritance tax. There has been speculation for years that this scheme would be closed and Labour identified it as an abuse, but it remains a legal tax-saving device".

David Miliband has consistently refused to comment. As well he might.

Iain Dale's Diary, www.iaindale.blogspot.com

New Labour Sleaze in . . .

2005

Gordon and Tony's Sleazeometer, 2005

17 sleazy episodes: Very Sleazy Guys

Cherie Coins it Down Under
John Angliss

It must be coincidence that Cherie Blair is mentioned so often in this book despite the powers of white witchcraft and Catholicism she has summoned to protect her. To honour this one-woman *Da Vinci Code*, the tale of her Australian speaking tour in 2005 must be told. Tickets to hear the First Lady of Downing Street cost between £75 and £4,100 and "100% of the profits" were to go to the Children's Cancer Institute Australia. An uncharacteristically generous gesture from Cherie.

Shortly afterwards, *The Times* published a draft budget which proved that this was entirely correct. The only snag was the small matter of the £102,000 of expenses which would go straight into the pockets of Cherie and her agent as a flat fee for the tour. This not only meant that those who paid out their cash for charity felt cheated, but also that the very future of the charity itself was put in jeopardy. Since only 8 per cent of gross earnings (£6,690) from the event reached the charity, it was in breach of its licence. It has since been resuscitated.

Having made enough PR mistakes during the Peter Foster/Cheriegate, it is interesting to note that Downing Street refused to comment throughout this debacle. Indeed, the whole tour turned into a PR nightmare for Cherie herself, exemplified when in New Zealand she addressed the crowds as "Australians".

According to *The Times*, a further speaking arrangement in Melbourne generated £6,774 for charity and £17,000 for the speaker. Small change for Cherie.

http://jangliss.livejournal.com

Pants "Not on Fire"
Wat Tyler

J ust what does it take to make your pants catch fire? Steve "Pants" Byers was determined to find out. In June 2001 he took a job as Transport Secretary and set about it. First he got his Departmental team secretly working up radical restructuring options for Railtrack, a privatised company he'd taken a fancy to.

He then forced Railtrack into administration so he could renationalise it on the cheap. Dispossessed share-holders were outraged, 50,000 of them suing him for *administrative misfeasance*, last seen in 1703.

Finally he appeared before the Commons Transport Sub-Committee and brazenly denied he'd pre-planned any of it: "Was there any discussion, theoretical or otherwise, in your Department... about the possibility of a future change in status for Railtrack, whether nationali-sation, the move into a company limited by guarantee, or whatever?" Byers: "Not that I am aware of."

Terrific play. But amazingly, despite a burning sensation around his crotch, his Calvins failed to ignite – later inspection revealed only a singed gusset. Everybody was very kind and *said* he was a liar, but that's not the same as actually having blazing pants. Disillusioned, he resigned.

As it turned out, he needn't have worried. In July 2005 those angry shareholders invited him to the High Court for a grilling. And there, confronted with stacks of evidence that he'd told a monstrous porkie to the Committee, his pants finally began smoldering: "It is true to say there was work going on, so, yes, that was untrue… It was such a long time ago, I cannot remember, but it is not a truthful statement… I cannot remember the motives behind it."

"Cannot remember" – brilliant stuff. In October 2005, he finished it with a personal statement to the Commons claiming he *had* now remembered: "the commissioning of work… on future options did not represent discussions in the true meaning of that word."

The old semantics one-two: superb. He sat down in triumph, evil yellow smoke belching from his rear vent. All he needed now was official authentication from the House Standards Committee.

But, incredibly, the Committee ruled against him. Yes, he'd been "factually inaccurate". Yes, he'd done it "for political reasons". And yes, he'd been "unwise" to concoct his retrospective justification. But, no, technically, his pants were "not on fire".

This is plainly ludicrous. We all *saw* the smoke, and Pants deserves proper recognition. We demand the matter be referred to the Guinness Book of Records.

Burning Our Money, www.burningourmoney.blogspot.com

Because She's Worth It
Paul Sorene

Why did you vote Labour at the 2005 General Election? Was it the Party's stance on the NHS, the leader's relationship with Cliff Richard? Or was it something else? Was it Cherie Blair's hair?

During the 2005 election campaign, the Labour Party was asked to pay £7,700 to secure the services of Cherie's personal hairstylist. The crimper's name was Andre Suard, and for £275 a day between 6th April and 6th May 2005 he strove to make Cherie look good enough to woo your vote.

Not that she was standing for Parliament – she unsuccessfully stood for Parliament in the 1980s; she was applying for the job of First Lady. As Peter Kilfoyle, a backbench Labour MP, said: "We are almost accepting by stealth a First Lady."

This was nonsense. There was nothing stealthy about it. American magazines have often referred to Cherie as the first lady. She was billed as "The trail-blazing first lady of Downing Street" when on her lucrative speaking tour in the States. And Cherie did not object.

And Cherie's hair has form, to go with that 'because-I'm-worth-it bounce'. Suard has accompanied Cherie on trips to Indonesia, Australia and the United States.

Sir Christopher Meyer, Britain's former ambassador to Washington, recalled in his memoirs one brush with Cherie's stylist. "Suddenly," says Meyer, "the cry went up: Cherie's hairdresser is missing! Her French stylist had accompanied us on our mission... He had been left behind at Camp David. A US marines helicopter brought him post-haste... as the rest of us kicked our heels."

But why should we care? As a spokesman for the party told us: "So what? Mrs Blair worked fantastically hard during the election and visited more than 50 constituencies during the campaign. She is enormously popular with the party and, don't forget, we won the election." So the two things are linked. It was the hair wot won it.

Over seven grand on hair does seem a lot, but when viewed as part of the race for power, it is cheap. And represents far better value than buying, say, a peerage. As Lord Suard of Barnet can only agree.

Anorak, www.anorak.co.uk

" CHEAPER IN THE LONG RUN, MADAM "

Cherie Goes to Washington
Chris Doidge

Cherie Blair – (or Booth when it suits her) – called in to question the 'spirit' of the Ministerial Code of Conduct in June 2005, when she seemingly benefited from her role as the Prime Minister's wife to the tune of over £30,000.

Blair – sorry, Booth – claimed her trip was unrelated to her time spent as Tony's consort, yet advertised a lecture she gave in Washington as an irresistible opportunity to hear from the "First Lady of Downing Street".

It seems unlikely that a lecture given by any other well-known QC would have attracted such a crowd, nor provided a pay-check for somewhere north of £30,000. And Mrs Blair/Booth's fee didn't include the royalties she earned from her book *The Goldfish Bowl: Married to the Prime Minister 1955-1997*.

While the Ministerial Code doesn't include the spouses of Ministers, Cherie's foray into highly-paid lecturing wasn't exactly in the spirit of the rule which states that ministers "should not accept payment for speeches of an official nature or which directly draw on their responsibilities or experience".

Arguably, given that Cherie and Tony probably share a bank account, Mr Blair himself probably benefited from the speech. His defence was that Norma Major never declared how much she made from a book on the PM's official residence, Chequers.

But criticism came from all sides. Peter Kilfoyle, the Labour backbencher said he thought the rules governing MPs' conduct were being applied more strongly for those at the bottom of the 'greasy pole' than those at the top.

And although Cherie's travel costs were paid privately (well, she can just about afford it with annual earnings from Matrix Chambers of circa £250,000), the Conservatives' Chris Grayling said, "There is no doubt in my mind that the Prime Minister and Mrs Blair have broken the spirit of the rules, if not the rules themselves." But calls for reform of the Code met with little response from Number 10.

Cherie's trip coincided with a trip by her husband to the very same city, although in one of the least plausible statements ever made by the Prime Minister's Official Spokesman, reporters were told that "If she and the Prime Minister are in Washington at the same time it is a coincidence."

Controversy-prone Cherie will probably chuckle that her hefty fee (merely a small portion of the Blairs' numerous mortgages) will have brought her long-term gain at the expense of short-term sleaze.

www.chrisdoidge.com

Cherie Blair (Not) Cutting the Ribbon
Shaun Rolfe

On 16th June 2005 the *Guardian* reported: "In a [strange] coincidence, it seems that Cherie Booth's visit next month to Kuala Lumpur, where she will deliver a law lecture and attend a breast cancer charity gala, will coincide with the relaunch of the duty free shopping complex Starhill, where the gala will take place. In preparation for this great occasion, each of the mall's seven floors has been given an enticing new name: Feast, Indulge, Adorn, Explore, Pamper, Relish and Muse.

In yet another coincidence, Starhill's owner, a Malaysian magnate called Francis Yeoh, has pointed out that the 'global arbiters of taste and style' whose shops now ornament his refurbished mall include 'Eric Way, the young and exciting couture designer, [who] dresses high-profile clients like Cherie Blair, Ivana Trump, Shirley Bassey...' As for Way, he has told a journalist that Mrs Blair will wear one of his dresses to the gala, where her fellow guests, according to the organisers, will include Dame Shirley Bassey and possibly, Ivana Trump.

As the devout Yeoh has pointed out in another context, 'All of mankind today is spun together in a complex web of interdependence. The consequence of interdependence is that we have a stake in each other's economic well-being.' Yeoh, for example, has a stake in Wessex Water.

Why shouldn't Mrs Blair's visit further the interests of the Malaysian economy? Or, at least, that large part of the Malaysian economy that belongs to Yeoh's YTL conglomerate, where the guiding philosophy is: 'World Class Products and Services at Third World Prices'? No reason, except that Yeoh's business thinking is not yet universally applied, with the result that some people are asking, with even more intensity than they asked last week, if Mrs Blair has taken leave of her senses."

Ten days later a Downing Street spokesman told reporters that Cherie Blair would not now attend the opening of the shopping mall due to "scheduling issues".

"They've all been disinvited. He doesn't want any British celebrities or press there," said Eric Way, the couturier who introduced Cherie to Mr Yeoh.

At the same briefing, in what was reported as a coordinated move to end criticism of Mrs Blair's money-making, the Number 10 spokesman said that Mrs Blair would donate to charity the fee from the forthcoming Channel 4 documentary based on her book *The Goldfish Bowl*. How gracious of her.

Play it Again, Richard
Tom Barry

Richard Bowker is an interesting example of how far a judicious bit of networking can take you. A fine pianist, in 2002, shortly after moving from Virgin Rail to head the Strategic Rail Authority, he accompanied the Prime Minister's guitar at a private birthday party. The logic of appointing someone from one of the chief troublemakers in the rail industry, whose grandiose plans were swallowing billions of pounds of taxpayers' money, is questionable; Virgin benefited from millions in subsidy from the SRA during Bowker's reign there, paying for the extra costs associated with their new trains, which he'd ordered. These are less efficient, of lower capacity, cause more damage to the track and require more staff. The result was predictable: in 2003/4 Virgin's Cross Country franchise should have received £50 million in subsidy and falling; the reality was a cool £250 million after a steep increase as Bowker's vision took wing.

The man at the top, by now combining the Chief Executive and Chairman role, was unbowed and in another musical interlude, he sang perfectly off the same hymn sheet as Tony Blair and Alistair Darling. Over three days in mid-2003 each man made a startlingly similar speech blaming "long-term underinvestment" for spiralling rail costs, missing the more obvious point that the structure of the industry inevitably resulted in increased cost.

By 2004, however, a note of disharmony came in. Virgin's Cross Country franchise was effectively cancelled and taken back into State control, with Virgin managing it for a percentage of income. Bowker admitted that costs were out of control, partly because of the overruns on the West Coast scheme he had helped devise back at Virgin. The Department for Transport starting planning to throw him out of his job.

The 2005 Railways Act abolished the SRA after four years in which it had done nothing except perpetuate the inefficient and costly bureaucracy of privatisation and add its own layer. In a final twist, 150 SRA civil servants continued to turn up to work for six months after the SRA's abolition.

However, all was not lost for Richard. In the big final number of the musical, he was rewarded for the abolition of his organisation with the CBE, and for his expertise in handing out vast sums of taxpayers' money by being made Chief Executive of Partnerships for Schools, spending £40 billion of your money on school PFI deals to create Tony Blair's 'legacy'.

The 'Terrorist' Heckler Pensioner
Tom Paine

The Walter Wolfgang incident is a small, perfect emblem of New Labour. Mr Wolfgang, an escapee from Nazism, is a long-time member of the Labour Party. He is an old-fashioned 'peace activist', more in keeping with the Party's Michael Foot epoch than with the glossy hardness of Blair and Brown. For him to frighten a fly, the insect would have to be of a rather nervous disposition. At the Labour Party's 2005 annual conference, in the best rough-and-tumble traditions of British debate, he shouted "nonsense" (or something to that effect) during a speech by the then Foreign Secretary, Jack Straw. In a rational world, he would have won a prize for staying awake in such trying circumstances and making a statement of the bleedin' obvious.

Straw is as weak an orator as he is a sex symbol (however much he wanted to be both when around Condoleeza Rice or various Blair Babes). Instead, in the irrational world we actually inhabit, Wolfgang was seized and forcibly ejected by the Party's hired thugs/security guards. So fragile is the connection between the "People's Party" and any actual people it encounters these days, the frail old geezer seems to have frightened the men of power. After his unseemly ejection, "Wolfie" (as he is known in Leftist circles) was arrested by police using "anti-terrorist" powers.

New Labour has lavished such powers on the police throughout its time in office. In theory, they are to protect us against the dark forces of terrorism. In fact, they are more to do with outflanking the Conservative Party on its traditional "safe ground" of law and order. "You want to hang them high? We will hang them higher!" (or rather fire seven head shots into them as they travel innocently to work). Libertarians have squawked in protest, but have been written off as mere "liberati" by such moral giants as David Blunkett. We warned darkly that new police powers would be used in ways that voters never imagined. Certainly, few imagined they would be used to harass frail old Labourites raising a quavering voice of dissent.

It was a tiny incident. Wolfie lives, unharmed; basking a little in his moment of fame. Blair's apology has been accepted. Too old to learn new tricks, Wolfie remains the naive socialist he has always been. But the curtain had slipped and we all had a small glimpse of our future.

The Last Ditch, http;//lastditch.typepad.com

Masters of False Reality
Justin McKeating

Proof that New Labour is the greatest political party in history was presented by Channel 4's *Dispatches* on 23rd May 2005. Not content with three historic election victories, bringing democracy to Iraq and the elevation of a priapic blind man to one of the great offices of state, New Labour can conjure worlds of their own imagining from the raw firmament.

The programme showed that the party is adept at creating what *Sky News*'s Political Editor, Adam Boulton, called a "false reality".

Propaganda techniques used by US pharmaceutical companies and political parties – known as "astroturfing" – were imported. Letters written by press officers praising New Labour or attacking the opposition were sent to activists who were told to get them into the local press. Identical letters appeared in newspapers across the country. One appeared in the same newspaper twice. In Leeds, letters were printed from a woman who didn't exist.

Fake demonstrations were organised to follow the leaders of the opposition parties and disrupt walkabouts and rallies. Outside the Tory's spring conference in Brighton, New Labour activists organised what was meant to look like a "spontaneous" protest by members of the public. The 'homemade' banners made no mention of Labour affiliations. Standing front and centre in the crowd was the New Labour candidate, and now MP, for Hove, Celia Barlow.

Throughout the New Labour campaign, the national media was bypassed almost completely with only TV cameras and local press invited to events. After Blair was ambushed by Nick Robinson at a poster launch, care was taken not to let it happen again. At the next event, once the cameras had got pictures for the evening news, party workers were corralled in front of reporters to prevent them getting to Blair. He shook hands with "endorsers", people billed as "ordinary voters and a cross section of the local community". In reality they were carefully chosen (black, Jewish, pensioners, families) to present the right image. These endorsers were endlessly recycled at different events.

Adam Boulton spoke of Blair's "sterile environment". Robinson wondered whether Blair had met a single real member of the electorate during the campaign, isolated as he was, from another Sharon Storer, the distraught partner of a cancer sufferer who had accosted him during the 2001 campaign. Did Blair or Brown realise they were meeting "voters" they'd "met" at other events, some of whom were party workers? Did they know they were making small talk with people handpicked because they were telegenic or fitted an ethnic demographic?

Boulton was generous and described Blair as "above it". But Blair was only one level removed, with Alastair Campbell and Alan Milburn "high-fiving" (as a *Dispatches* undercover reporter witnessed) in the press office.

Chicken Yoghurt, www.chickyog.net

Moneygrabbing
Phil Hendren

L ike the colour of their logo, New Labour has been in the red with their bank manager for a while. Those pre-election loans in 2005 certainly didn't help move the books into the black. The debt problems might help explain why Labour HQ decided to start charging £200 for information requests about their Prospective Parliamentary Candidates (PPCs) back in March 2005.

If you're wondering what sort of information I mean, it's their CVs. You know the sort of stuff, what school you went to – Fettes for example. Your experiences of real work – I stress "real". Or the other usual lies you put in CVs such as "I support Newcastle United". Now you may very well think that this is not a major scandal. After all, £200 doesn't sound like a lot of money, but what if you were a voter who wanted to know about PPC? Suddenly you're told you need to pay for information that you have a right to know?

It's very simple, if you're going to stand for Parliament – like one of the editors of this book did – then you're entering PUBLIC life. That means you let the public know about you openly when they ask and to hell with the consequences.

The fact that Labour wanted to charge for access to this information means they were either seriously stuck for cash (possible); many of their candidates had more skeletons in their cupboards than Alan Clark (feasible); or they're just a bunch of money grabbers (likely). Or all three. You decide.

Dizzy Thinks http://dizzythinks.net

Bullying Journalists
Iain Dale

lastair Campbell is renowned for bullying journalists and for his foul, sleazy mouth. If we ever
had any doubt about the matter, all we need do is
look at the extracts from his diaries which he was forced
to make public during the Hutton Inquiry. One particularly charming extract reads: "I agreed it would fuck
Gilligan if that [Dr Kelly] was his source."

But an even better example came in an email
containing a four-letter outburst aimed at BBC journalists. Mr Campbell sent the email by mistake to BBC2's
Newsnight after it questioned his role in Labour's controversial campaign posters.

He later emailed the show saying the original email
had been sent in error and that it was all a "silly fuss".
Campbell messaged *Newsnight* after the programme
investigated claims that Labour's advertising agency
TBWA was blaming him for the brouhaha over its
campaign posters. The images, including one of flying
pigs and another of what critics claim depicted Tory
leader Michael Howard as Fagin, prompted accusations
of anti-Semitism. Mr Campbell's email, which was apparently intended for a party official, suggested they should
get Trevor Beattie, TBWA's MD, to issue a statement.

In the email Alastair Campbell said: "Just spoke to trev.
think tbwa shd give statement to newsnight saying party

and agency work together well and nobody here has spoken to standard. Posters done by by tbwa according to political brief. Now fuck off and cover something important you twats!" The email was sent by mistake to *Newsnight* journalist Andrew McFadyen. Realising his error, Mr Campbell then emailed Mr McFadyen pointing out the mistake, but suggesting presenter Jeremy Paxman would have seen the funny side. He said: "Not very good at this email Blackberry malarkey. Just looked at log of sent messages, have realised email meant for colleagues at TBWA has gone to you. For the record, first three sentences of email spot on. No row between me and trevor. Posters done by them according to our brief. I dreamt up flying pigs. Pigs not great but okay in the circs of Tories promising tax cuts and spending rises with the same money. TBWA made production. Campbell swears shock. Final sentence of earlier email probably a bit colourful and personal considering we have never actually met but I'm sure you share the same sense of humour as your star presenter Mr P. Never known such a silly fuss since the last silly fuss but there we go. Must look forward not back." Indeed we must.

Iain Dale's Diary, www.iaindale.blogspot.com

The Union Modernisation Fund
Matthew Sinclair

L abour is facing a fairly serious funding crisis. Thanks to this crisis it is dependent upon the generous support of the unions. Unfortunately the unions aren't rolling in cash either. Their membership has been in decline for some time as people move out of highly unionised industries and into the service sector. It is at precisely this moment when the whole house of loan-slips threatens to come crashing down that the Union Modernisation Fund, a vehicle for the Labour government to give £10 million of taxpayer money to the unions over three years, is created. Such a coincidence makes people cynical. The department responsible for the plan, the Department of Trade and Industry, makes clear that this money cannot be used for political projects. Unfortunately, the unions, like most organisations, have limitations on their budget and their membership's willingness to pay expanded dues. If the Government is willing to pay for Amicus to communicate with its branches then more of the income that comes from its members is likely to be sent the Labour Party's way. It is for this reason that Frances Maude called this plan "very, very direct sleaze. That is buying influence and buying taxpayers' money". The Metropolitan Police are apparently investigating.

Some of the scheme's supporters counter that, as money is also given to unions who do not fund the

Labour Party, this is not a scheme designed to reward supporters. Unfortunately, all that suggests is that the Labour Party doesn't mind spreading taxpayer money around a little in order to make the sleaze a little less brutally obvious.

The decline of the unions is a process which places the Labour Party in crippling financial difficulties thanks to the Party's inability to raise funds from an increasingly disillusioned membership. That it is intervening and providing government support to a lobby group which acts only in its own interests rather than the national interest is a scandal. It is of course a clear 'result' for trade union and Labour Party treasurers.

Sinclair's Musings, http://sinclairsmusings.blogspot.com

It Pays to Talk
Guido Fawkes

T he Official Labour Election Night Party in May 2005, held at the National Portrait Gallery, and organised by PR guru Matthew Freud, at a cost of £50,000 (paid for personally by Charlie Dunstone, the Carphone Warehouse multi-millionaire). It was attended by Lord Levy, the Labour fundraiser. David Campbell, chief executive of the Anschutz Entertainment Group was another guest. He is now set to make millions by bringing gambling to the Millennium Dome, thanks to Labour's relaxing of the gaming laws. The takeover of the disastrous Dome was itself politically controversial, with allegations flying about of influence peddling.

Charles Dunstone, chief executive of Carphone Warehouse, claimed the Labour Party tried to bounce him into making a £1m donation. Dunstone, who is a fan of Tony Blair but not of Labour, said he was "nobbled" by Lord Levy, the party's sleazy fundraiser.

"I saw Lord Levy walk past me," said the owner of Talk Talk "Then he spun round, came back and said: 'You are Charles Dunstone, aren't you?' I said yes. He said: 'Good. Can we put you down for a million?'" Dunstone tried to brush off the "extraordinary" comment but the ever persistent man dubbed "Lord Cashpoint" eventually extracted his business card from him. The centi-millionaire founder of the mobile phone giant admitted that

Lord Levy's flippant approach was serious. Dunstone later wrote to the party's general secretary expressing his outrage at the approach, saying he has no plans to donate money to Labour or any other party. "I don't feel comfortable doing it and I think if you're a person closely associated with any business it's a bad thing to do. It's bad to align your organisation with a political organisation." Charlie Dunstone knew better than to risk repelling his millions of individual customers by becoming notorious as a Labour-backing business tycoon, or possibly since his business does not rely on government contracts or influence, he was immune to Lord Levy's charming menace.

Guido Fawkes www.order-order.com

Candy Atherton's Opposition 'Research'
Simon Maybin

The folk in deepest Cornwall are not famed for their open-mindedness. So when Paul Phillips, researcher for the Labour MP for Falmouth & Camborne Candy Atherton, felt he was being asked by his employer to "look into" stories about the local Tory candidate's gay lifestyle, Phillips was understandably uncomfortable.

It didn't help matters that Phillips himself was openly gay, and felt he was expected to use his 'insider knowledge' of the London scene to dig up some dirt.

Candy Atherton told Phillips of a press story she had seen about Ashley Crossley. She recounted the tale – laughing as she told it, according to Phillips – of how Crossley had been held at knifepoint. Atherton, Phillips alleged, wanted her researcher to find out more. He walked out.

Phillips brought an employment tribunal claim against Atherton for discrimination and harassment on the grounds of sexual orientation. At the hearing Atherton admitted asking her researcher to find out about Crossley, her Tory opponent, but said she "would not want any personal political gain because of other people's prejudice".

The claim was eventually thrown out because it had been made too late, although the panel also said it did not accept parts of Phillips's story.

Of course being a journo by trade, Candid Candy could have had no idea how these kinds of revelations would have played with the Cornwall electorate. On her website – under the heading 'Family Life' – Atherton happily informs readers that in 2001 she "married her long-term partner, Cornishman Broderick Ross".

As it turned out, the publicity wasn't great for either candidate come the general election. Atherton was booted out by LibDem media 'dahling' Julia Goldsworthy in the May 2005 vote. Crossley, who had also suffered from some vicious homophobia at the hands of his local constituency party, came a close third.

Labour and Unison Breach Electoral Laws in Unison?
Damon Lambert

It's hard to know quite where the Labour Party ends and Unison begins. As Gordon Brown said after the 2005 general election: "I thank UNISON because, under Dave Prentis' leadership, and with the campaign you mounted, the national posters warning of the threat of the Tory party; the 300,000 direct mailings that you sent to people in key constituencies; the trade union co-ordinators you provided in 43 of the key seats that we were fighting; and the vital work you did targeting these marginals; without your work, we would not have won. That is why I am so grateful to you."

According to the Electoral Commission's records, UNISON donations to Labour during the election were £24,493. Staff costs were £6,707. If UNISON provided 43 staff then they must have paid on average £155 for over four weeks' work. What a scandal, UNISON does not even pay minimum wage! If the rest of the donation is assumed to be the 300,000 direct mailings then UNISON must be congratulated on going to the post office and managing to buy 300,000 rare six-pence stamps, with presumably a whole load of paper, envelopes and printing ink chucked in for free.

Section 50 of the the Political Parties, Elections and Referendums Act ("PPERA") considers donations to include any paying of expenses incurred directly or indirectly by the party, the provision otherwise than on commercial terms of any property, services or facilities for the use or benefit of the party (including the services of any person). Examples are shown clearly in the guidelines.

As Gordon Brown is meant to be a stickler for detail may be his Labour Party colleagues would like to bear in mind the relevant section of the PPERA.:

Section 61. – (1) A person commits an offence if he-
(a) knowingly enters into, or
(b) knowingly does any act in furtherance of, any arrangement which facilitates or is likely to facilitate, whether by means of any concealment or disguise or otherwise, the making of donations to a registered party by any person or body other than a permissible donor

Taxcutter, http://.thetaxcutter.blogspot.com

The Second Resignation of David Blunkett MP

Gregor Hopkins

David Blunkett's second resignation illustrates just how far removed from reality long-serving Cabinet Ministers can become. They think they're omnipotent. They believe whatever they do they can get away with. They become remote from the 'little people' as their ministerial Jaguars shuttle them from pillar to post. But events catch up with them in the end and it is in this light that we must view Blunkett's second ignoble resignation.

The circumstances leading up to 'second resignation' day on 2nd November 2005 are well documented. A year previously he had left Blair's Cabinet in disgrace over 'Nannygate' and was continuing his public spat with ex-mistress Kimberly Quinn over their illegitimate child. Perhaps it is understandable that Mr B took his eye off the ball and went onto achieve his spectacular 'double'.

In March 2005 the one-time leading socialist and hater of capitalism David Blunkett bought shares in DNA Biosciences and was made a non-executive director of the company. In itself this posed no problem and shouldn't have caused any eyebrows to be raised unduly. But following the 2005 election Tony Blair decided to appoint Blunkett to be Secretary of State for Work & Pensions, a Department in which DNA Biosciences was bidding for lucrative contracts. If those contracts came to fruition Blunkett stood to make a shed load of money. The problem was that David Blunkett hadn't registered his directorships properly.

Unfortunately, a grey area in the parliamentary system is that following the dissolution of Parliament, prior to a General Election, the country has no Parliament and no MPs. Therefore, strictly speaking, Blunkett didn't need to register his little money spinner. Although he did let it be known that he had bought the shares, he didn't register them with the Cabinet Secretary at the time. Furthermore, and perhaps fatally for his career, he didn't respond to any of the three (yes, three) letters from the Advisory Committee on Business Appointments which advised him to seek committee approval for his venture.

Though warned that these shares presented a startling conflict of interest, Blunkett soldiered on – a bit of fobbing here, a declaration of innocence there. But in the end it all caught up with him. Sir Alistair Graham, chairman of the Committee on Standards in Public Life proclaimed that he had breached the ministerial code, which in effect meant the game was up. He handed in his resignation but from his subsequent statements you could tell he couldn't quite see what he had done wrong. The whole episode left one with a distinct feeling of déjà vu.

The Blog, www.gregor.org.uk

Taking Liberties
Jonathan Sheppard

The Labour Government is full of contradiction with this fact being most apparent in the area of civil liberties. On the one hand they have singularly failed to stamp down on anti-social behaviour, yet at the same time they have presided over the biggest erosion of civil liberties of the law-abiding majority ever seen in the history of our country. The Government suggests ID cards are required for the war against terrorism, yet who could trust a Labour Government whose control freakery in the past has led to an 82-year-old heckler, Walter Wolfgang, being ejected from the Labour Conference, and one of their own MPs, Austin Mitchell, having his camera seized and his pictures deleted.

More recently this constant obsession at controlling our lives led to a 25-year-old vegan cook from Hastings being found guilty of breaching Section 132 of the new Serious Organised Crime and Police Act. She was arrested in October for reading names of soldiers killed in Iraq at central London's Cenotaph.

What does this tell us about the country we live in? Don't disagree – because if you do they will introduce a law which makes it illegal. Don't protest – or you could go to jail. Don't go off message, even if you are a Labour MP – or suffer the consequences. Civil liberties have to be protected, but Labour sees them as just another added complication whose erosion is a price worth paying. Is this sleaze? Surely the curtailment of freedom of speech using legislation which we were promised would never be used improperly is the ultimate betrayal.

Tory Radio, www.toryradio.com

New Labour Sleaze in . . .

2006

Gordon and Tony's Sleazeometer, 2006

32 sleazy episodes: Help! Police!

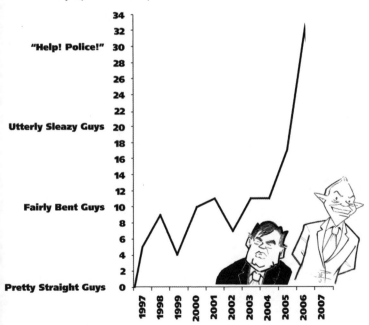

"Help! Police!" — 30

Utterly Sleazy Guys — 20

Fairly Bent Guys — 10

Pretty Straight Guys — 0

34 32 30 28 26 24 22 20 18 16 14 12 10 8 6 4 2 0

1997 1998 1999 2000 2001 2002 2003 2004 2005 2006 2007

An 'Inadvertent Error'
Bel Andrew

U ntil his recent fall from grace, the Deputy Prime Minister, John Prescott, was the Cabinet minister in charge of council tax. Taxpayers are struggling under the rising burden of this most unfair of local taxes. Pensioners on fixed incomes are among the hardest hit. Annual council tax increases outstrip the rate of inflation. Appeals for relief fall on deaf ears, and pensioners are being jailed for non-payment. Not all tax-dodging old people are treated in this way, though. It was revealed in January 2006 that 67-year-old Prescott had not paid a single council tax bill since 1997 for his plush grace-and-favour flat in Admiralty Arch. The taxpayer paid his total bill of £3,830.52. He says it was all a mistake, an "inadvertent error" by his staff. Poor lamb. He thought that the tax was deducted along with his income tax. Since when is council tax collected through PAYE? Perhaps somebody (a real pensioner, maybe) could try that defence in court: "Sorry m'lud, I thought my council tax had been deducted from my already meagre pension", etc. Anyway, since when was ignorance a defence?

In addition the flat was incorrectly classed as his "secondary" residence, thereby qualifying for a discount. So the actual tax due should have been much higher than £3,830.52. Mr Prescott again claimed ignorance, blaming this on the previous Conservative administration.

He has promised to refund the money, and ordered that future bills be sent directly to him. Perhaps a little late.

Margaret Beckett's Air Miles
Andrew Woodman

Margaret Beckett is the ex-Bennite ex-deputy leader of the Labour Party, ex-Secretary of State at the Department of the Environment and now our first female and first caravanning Foreign Secretary.

When she was Secretary of State for the Environment, her department's website stated: "Mrs Beckett leads for the UK in international negotiations on sustainable development and climate change". She was therefore, the Government leader on 'going green'.

Reconcile this with the admission that Margaret Beckett took 106 RAF flights between 2002 and December 2004 whilst in that role. Yes, to travel the 130 miles between the DEFRA office to the city of Derby, the woman in charge of the Environment rejected the train (station three miles from her home) and instead took the RAF Squadron 32 to East Midlands Airport (13 miles away from her home). The monetary cost of all this being allegedly only a notional £107,000. The National Audit Office estimates the actual cost to be more like £1m. A shocking use and waste of public money. One wonders how she tipped the pilot.

However, it doesn't end there. Consider this report from the BBC: "The UK is unlikely to meet its target of reducing CO_2 emissions by 20% by 2010, a Government report says. 'The Climate Change Programme review projects that new and existing policies will deliver a cut of 15-18% by the end of the decade. Environment Secretary Margaret Beckett said the government was not giving up on meeting the 20% goal, but said more had to be done to reach it. The review encourages people to cut their personal emissions.'"

Will she practise what she used to preach now she is Foreign Secretary? A nation waits to find out.

Real Power to the People
http://realpowertothepeople.blogspot.com

Fancy a Peerage, Boyo?

Peter Henn

Blaenau Gwent was the seat Labour would never lose. A seat held, in various incarnations, by Nye Bevan and Michael Foot. So, in 2005, Labour promptly lost it. The local Labour Party wanted Assembly Member and former council leader Peter Law to replace Llew Smith. The national Labour Party announced they weren't going to listen to BGCLP and insisted on having an all-woman shortlist, much to the chagrin of many local members, who promptly tore up their membership cards in protest. Now, if you were a Labour supporter, who would you trust? The people who gave Parliament the likes of Bevan and Foot, or the people who decided that Ron Davies, the badger's friend, should be put in charge of Wales?

After wrestling with his conscience Peter Law decided to stand against the official Labour candidate and to everyone's astonishment he overturned a Labour majority of 19,000 with a majority of his own of more than 9,000.

It was too good to last. In April 2006 Mr Law, who in the meantime had become one of the most popular constituency MPs in the country, lost his battle with cancer. Before he was even buried, Labour HQ had started canvassing for the coming by-election.

A week after his death Peter Law's widow Trish gave an interview to the Welsh political programme *Dragon's Eye*.

She duly announced that a "senior" Labour figure had offered her husband a peerage if he agreed not to stand in the election. The Labour Party press machine swung into action and immediately denied any wrongdoing. A week later, on local election polling day, Plaid Cymru leader Elfyn Llwyd MP accused Welsh Secretary Peter Hain of doing the dirty deed. Even worse for Labour, he alleged under the cloak of parliamentary privilege that it had all happened with the authority of the Prime Minister.

A postscript: Maggie Jones was given a peerage in the 2006 Honours list, no doubt for "services to the Labour Party". She had contrived to lose the safest Labour seat in Wales. Makes you long for an elected second chamber, doesn't it?

Red Ken's Standards Found Wanting
Andrew Ian Dodge

On 24th February 2006 London Mayor Ken Livingston lost his appeal against suspension by The Adjudication Panel for England when they upheld the Board of Deputies of British Jews' complaint, that Ken comparing an *Evening Standard* reporter, Oliver Feingold, to a "concentration camp guard" brought his office into disrepute. To quote the panel which passed the one-month ban (on full pay): "The case tribunal is, however, concerned that the Mayor does seem to have failed, from the outset of this case, to have appreciated that his conduct was unacceptable, was a breach of the code [the GLA code of conduct] and did damage to the reputation of his office."

They went on to say it was "unnecessarily insensitive and offensive".

Ken and his supporters protested, believing that the voters of London were the only ones able to remove him from the office of Mayor. The exchange between the Mayor and the *Evening Standard* reporter occurred outside a party celebrating the twentieth anniversary of Chris Smith, former Islington MP, declaring his homosexuality. The exchange was caught on tape which was played to the panel and widely distributed in both the media and online.

Ken Livingstone was recorded asking reporter Oliver Feingold if he is a "German war criminal". Mr Feingold replies: "No, I'm Jewish, I wasn't a German war criminal. I'm quite offended by that." The mayor then says: "Ah right, well you might be, but actually you are just like a concentration camp guard, you are just doing it because you are paid to, aren't you?"

Despite having written for the *Evening Standard* as a restaurant critic the Mayor excused his comments as being about the record of newspaper's owner, Associated Newspapers, during the 1930s. He felt their record during the 1930s justified his description of one of their reporters.

Ken's supporters reacted angrily to the ruling. Sir Iqbal Sacranie, the Secretary General of the Muslim Council of Britain, said: "This decision constitutes a clear over-reaction and an affront to our democratic traditions."

The ruling and four-week suspension from office – at the time of writing still subject to a judicial review brought by Livingstone – tarnished the Mayor's reputation for being welcoming and embracing to all of London's ethnic communities. The jibe was one of a string of dubious comments and behaviour regarding Jews in London. But, incredibly, such statements did not stop with the ruling – he has since made dubious comments about the Reuben brothers, who are Jewish, and their reluctance to sell land he wants for the 2012 Olympic project.

Dodgeblogium, www.andrewiandodge.com

Loans for Lordships
Jonathan Sheppard and Guido Fawkes

I n the spring of 2006 Blair's credibility with the public fell to new depths when the "Loans for Lordships" scandal hit the front pages and Scotland Yard launched a criminal investigation into political corruption. On a little-read blog belonging to Nick Bowes, the Labour Party's former Head of High Value Fundraising, he wrote on 21st March that "I have been minded to write an explosive entry about millionaire loans to the Labour Party for a while now".

The explosive entry, if it were ever to be written would have admitted that the serious allegations about loans being made to the Labour Party in return for seats in the House of Lords had substance. If it was an opposition politician making this allegation it would be written off as a party political spat, but when a former Labour staffer, an associate of Lord Levy, Blair's personal fundraiser, states on his own blog that "the whole peerages thing is corrupt", then questions have to be asked. Indeed Scotland Yard detectives are asking the questions of Lord Levy, the man nicknamed "Mr Cashpoint".

In the run-up to the last election the Labour Party secured loans of £14 million from wealthy business people including £1 million from Rod Aldridge, CEO of Capita. Capita is a firm with *billions* in government contracts so would be vulnerable to an approach from the Prime Minister's fundraiser. We all know you "do not to ask for credit because refusal often offends". What businessman would want to offend his biggest customer, even if as the Labour Party claims it was unlikely to make any real difference, would you as CEO want to risk offending the source of more than half your revenues? Rod Aldridge didn't approach Labour with an offer to help, they approached him – "The Labour Party came to me last year in need of financial support following the costs incurred at the last general election," he said. Businessmen are cynical about politicians, most would view such an approach as a shakedown, but what real choice would they have?

£2 million from Richard Caring, £1.5 million from Dr Chai Patel and £2 million from David Sainsbury, the Science minister who is reputed to have lent and given over £13 million to Labour. Lord Drayson, another Government minister, got his peerage weeks after giving £500,000 to Labour. Whilst there is nothing intrinsically wrong in loaning a political party money, there is certainly something wrong if it could be seen to be buying a seat in the legislature, so much so that Nick Bowes, who worked at the heart of the Labour Party, wrote, "I still think the crucial questions are a) why were donors persuaded to change their donations into loans and b) to what extent was the Prime Minister involved? In answer to a) you have to conclude it is because they were going to get peerages and Number 10 didn't want to draw a relationship between the two and b) the Prime Minister was in it up to his neck and was personally involved."

Are we to believe that the millions loaned were given in the expectation that there was nothing to come in return? Seventeen out of 22 individuals who have recently donated over £100,000 to Labour have been given an honour, and all but one who have donated more than £1 million has been given a peerage. Unsurprisingly, a YouGov poll showed 56 per cent of people believe Tony Blair gave peerages in exchange for loans and donations.

Barry Townsley made a loan of £1 million and was recommended for the Lords. Sir David Gerrard, a property developer, loaned the party around £2 million before he was put on the list for a peerage. Sleazy Levy, who mixes in the same social circles, would have known that they were risking hundreds of millions on a development getting Government planning approval from John Prescott, Gerrard would therefore be vulnerable to an approach from the Labour Party's fundraiser – well, if you have a £600 million property development resting on Government approval what is a £3 million "loan"? Both peerages were blocked by the Lord's Appointments Commission. Des Smith, a former council member of the Specialist Schools and Academies Trust (SSA Trust), which helps the Government to recruit sponsors for Blair's academies, told an undercover *Sunday Times* reporter that big financial donations to help set up the schools would guarantee a gong. He put it plainly: "the prime minister's office would recommend someone like [the donor] for an OBE, a CBE or a knighthood" .

Asked if this would be just for getting involved in the academies, he responded: "Yes ... they call them services to education. I would say to [the SSA Trust] office that we've got to start writing to the Prime Minister's office... you could go to the House of Lords". Des Smith's admission is *prima facie* evidence of what we all know. If you wanted a peerage, a seven-figure loan to the Labour Party and the same again donated to a city academy obtained it. Levy induced it. He covertly procured the money for the Labour Party.

Labour MP Austin Mitchell said "In the last election Tony panicked as usual... called Levy and said 'Get what it takes'. Which he did because he's brilliant at fund raising, So he went out on auto-beg and collected squillions for our first PFI election. Labour spent the lot (or rather chucked it away) and no one knew what was involved until now. Pity the bastard was so dependent on teenage geniuses..."

You have to ask why did the Labour Party treasurer Jack Dromey and other elected party officials know nothing about what was going on. It will be left to Deputy Assistant Commissioner John Yates, who is conducting a police investigation, to find out.

Tony Blair says he is delighted that business people support Labour. The rest of us, including his own MPs and former party workers, are left wondering why they do so.

Tory Radio, www.toryradio.com;
Guido Fawkes, www.order-order.com

Cameron Mackintosh's Nightmare
UK Paul

I n April 2006 the press reported that theatre magnate Cameron Mackintosh had been offered a peerage in return for a loan – an offer he very quickly refused. The stuff of which nightmares are made…

As he reflected on the offer of a Lordship in return for his loan to the Labour Party Cameron Mackintosh drifted off into sleep and into a dream ballet resembling one of his most popular productions. In that halfway house between wakefulness and oblivion there he stood, as the boy who asked for more, confronted by the looming figure of an elegantly coiffured man in a grey suit. "Please sir, all I want is a safer, cleaner West End," pleaded young Mackintosh. The man responded, with nary a mention of the problem of attracting theatregoers, but by breaking out into a lusty rendition of 'Lords for sale, going cheap, only a million quid." Surprised by this generous and unexpected offer but aware of its dubious legality Mackintosh backed away and escaped down Shaftesbury Avenue, dodging the dancing chimney sweeps and coster-mongers as best he could. As he passed through a deserted Whitehall he was observed by a sinister, shadowy figure who, as he passed, intoned that the only thing that counted in life was to have large amounts in the bank. Frightened that his pocket was in danger of being well and truly picked, and shocked that his charitable instincts were being compromised, he ran and hid in the shadow of the Palace of Westminster. There, at last, he found a welcoming face, "My name's Prescott," it said, "but people know me better as the 'Artless Bodger'". In their ensuing conversation Mackintosh related how he didn't expect anything in return for his generosity. "Are you daft? Everyone has their finger in the pies, even me and I ate most of mine!" "You want more?" Bodger said, "You've come to the right place."

Mackintosh jolted awake, the nightmare vision of a world where everything was tied to personal advancement fading quickly and thankfully away. The telephone rang soon after, the voice on the other end asking, "So how does Lord Mackintosh sound to you then?" The click of the receiver being replaced told that caller all he needed to know.

John Reid Goes to Pot
Iain Dale

What with John Prescott's affair, Charles Clarke's prisoner troubles and Patricia Hewitt being booed by nurses it was hard to believe that Tony Blair's May Day week could get any worse. But it did. Scottish Police announced they had discovered a small amount of cannabis in the home of the then Defence Secretary, Dr John Reid, during a regular security sweep.

In a bizarre coincidence Reid was in Afghanistan at the time of the discovery. The police helpfully made it clear that the cannabis could have been there for up to 20 years. The 'pot' was discovered in the guest room so Reid was conveniently able to make clear it must have belonged to someone else. The cannabis was said to weigh a gram and was worth 85p – that's £29 an ounce in real money. No explanation was given of the find. If it had been there for 20 years, why hadn't it been found before?

Were they going through the Reid sock drawer or was a sniffer dog being used? If it was a dog it must have been a very talented one because different dogs are used to find drugs and explosives. Dr Reid was very lucky indeed that the news was dominated by Prescott and Clarke. No one thought about what would happen to a serving soldier if cannabis was discovered in his house. It can safely be said that it would not be 'laughed off'. Six days later Dr Reid was promoted to the position of Home Secretary, where he now oversees our drugs policy. You couldn't make it up.

Rachel From North London
Chris Palmer

So just what does the Labour Party believe is an insult? Is it being accused of "sexing up" a dossier claiming that weapons of mass destruction could be used by Saddam Hussein in "45 minutes," or perhaps someone calling Tony Blair a liar, or even newspapers labelling the Labour Government "corruption and malicious"?

No, according to the Labour Party, these are just "false allegations" or "fabrications of the truth" (and Labour should know – they specialise in producing what many might label as lies, themselves). But no. In actual fact, according to our former Home Secretary Charles Clarke, this is an insult: "Congratulations on fixing the meeting so that nobody can ask questions! Well, I have a question. My daughter was feet away from the 7/7 King's Cross bomb, and she and some other survivors have said they are not angry with the bombers, but with the Government, because there was no public enquiry. Why is there no public enquiry?" To this spectacularly "insulting" question, Charles Clarke snarled, "Get away from me. I will not be insulted by you, this is an insult." Rachel from North London, the survivor of the King's Cross bombing and daughter of the questioner above commented, "Why is it an insult when the father of a bomb survivor, a gentle man of God, who has never caused trouble in his life, asks for a public enquiry? Why is his question not answered?" Indeed, why is this question unanswered and why was it so insulting? Is it because the question is unanswerable and asked in a rude or insulting manner? Or is it because like so many Labour Government ministers, Charles Clarke believes that his authority and word are infallible, and that those who seek to question his divine decisions are attempting to undermine and lessen his greatness?

To be fair to him, in the end Charles Clarke agreed to meet Rachel and her father and apologised to them, but Rachel is far from happy. Read about her experience at www.rachelnorthlondon.blogspot.com

www.chrispalmer.org

Tessa Jowell
Chris Mounsey

In early April 2006 a row erupted over the repayment of a mortgage taken out by Tessa Jowell, Minister for Culture, and her husband, international tax lawyer David Mills.

Four years before, the two had taken out a joint mortgage of £400,000 which was then paid off within a matter of weeks, apparently with the aid of a $600,000 (£344,000) gift from what Mr Mills described to his accountant as "B's people". This was assumed to refer to the then Italian Prime Minister, Silvio Berlusconi, for whom Mills had recently given favourable testimony in an alleged corruption case.

So, not only was the gift itself slightly suspect, but the way in which the gift had been dealt with raised more than an eyebrow. Tessa found herself under fire, and the explanation she offered was the most incredible part of the whole affair.

Tessa maintained ignorance of the gift and, more surprising still, was apparently unaware that the mortgage had been paid off.

That this assertion was treated with a certain amount of incredulity was most certainly not at all surprising. Despite her oh-so-onerous workload, the idea that Tessa had failed to spot the lack of mortgage statements for four years, as well as the concomitant pile of vital paperwork that would have arrived – addressed both to her and her husband – upon completion of the mortgage, seemed, frankly, a little far-fetched.

Tessa's case was referred, under the Ministerial Code, to the Cabinet Secretary, Sir Gus O'Donnell, who cleared her of any wrongdoing: "The important thing is that Tessa Jowell has accepted that he [her husband] should have done [told her about the money], has said she would have informed her permanent secretary if he had done so and explained the circumstances… By the time that she became aware that it had been reclassified as earnings he was paying tax on it and therefore under the rules it did not have to be declared if it is earnings which are being taxed."

Clear? Tessa meanwhile became the first Cabinet Minister to resign from her marriage to spend more time with her job.

Devil's Kitchen, http://devilskitchen.me.uk

"YOU LOOK DIFFERENT TODAY DAVID. HAVE YOU DONE SOMETHING WITH YOUR HAIR?"

The Tale of Two Shags and His Cocktail Sausage

Dipesh Palana

D on Juan, Casanova and Lord Byron are all names not usually linked with that of John Prescott. Although once described as an "inveterate macho", the image of a smooth, suave, sophisticated, serial seducer is scarcely compatible with the reality of the pugnacious corpulent bruiser of a Deputy Prime Minister, champion of the Labour working class, renowned for his mangled syntax and a seemingly resolute tendency to wind up with his foot in his mouth. All of that was to change in arguably Labour's worst week in office since the election of May '97.

In the week prior to the local government elections of April 2006, Labour was already facing catastrophe. Patricia Hewitt had been jeered by the Royal College of Nurses for claiming that the NHS had seen its best ever year, and Charles Clarke was close to resignation over his department's accidental release and subsequent loss of a then unknown number of dangerous foreign criminals. Westminster watchers could barely contain their delight then when the *Daily Mirror* revealed Prescott's affair with his diary secretary, 43-year-old Tracey Temple.

Almost immediately, a near torrent of other names came forward. Sarah Bissett-Scott claimed to have had a two year affair with Prescott some years previously, and allegations of several other potentially explosives affairs had yet to be confirmed at the time of writing. Tricia McDaid claimed to have been sexually harassed as a party aide and air stewardess Helga Forde claimed that her skin had crawled when Prescott ogled her breasts and said "lovely pair" as she served him fruit on a transatlantic flight. Linda McDougall, wife of MP Austin Mitchell, made allegations of having been groped as far back as 1978.

Particular mirth was had from rumours that Prescott, upon hearing that one of the affairs was to be reported, confessed to his wife Pauline first, but admitted to the wrong affair entirely. It was later revealed that had

Prescott not caved in and admitted to the *Mirror*'s initial allegations, they would have had a difficult time running with the story due to a lack of credible evidence. The affairs were particularly embarrassing given Prescott's previous pious stance on ethics and morality when criticising affairs by Conservative MPs in the Major years.

Prescott faced further problems when Ms Temple, with the help of PR guru Max Clifford, sold her story to the *Mail on Sunday*, giving a tearful television interview in the process. Questions were tabled in the Commons over a possible misuse of public finances when Prescott was found to have entertained Ms Temple at his official residence, and there was much consternation over the fact that Ms Temple was being paid out of the public purse, leading to a clear conflict of interest. Although the issue had struck a chord with voters on doorsteps, and despite being denounced by female Labour MPs, with Geraldine Smith accusing him of "the worst sort of abuse of power", he refused to resign and Blair refused to fire him.

Following the allegations in the *Mail on Sunday*, Prescott threatened to take the newspaper to the Press Complaints Commission. This was seen as unwise in many quarters, not least because he had in the past year referred to the chairman of the PCC, Sir Christopher Meyer, as a "red socked fop". Further damaging revelations showed that in fact the paper had been kind to Prescott by toning down the initial story, saying off the record that the original would have been "unsuitable for a family newspaper". This didn't stop blogger Iain Dale from leaking the unflattering details of the pulled story, which were then printed in the *Sun* on local election polling day. They involved Prescott's use of Viagra, which didn't always work, a comparison of the size of his appendage to a cocktail sausage, and Prescott's predilection for being naked and engaging in sexual relations within his office with the door open, as civil servants worked around them.

The accumulation of scandals led to Labour's worst local election showing for over 30 years. Although Blair went on to purge his Cabinet in a reshuffle the following day, Prescott somehow managed to cling on to the position of Deputy Prime Minister, thus keeping the trappings of a Cabinet Minister, but was stripped of all ministerial responsibilities. The decision was criticised from both sides of the Commons, and it is suspected that a deal was struck in which Prescott would acknowledge his role and shoulder some of the burden of Labour's electoral failure. It prompted the *Sun* to run with the headline "Now we're all being screwed by Prescott!" Ms Temple wasn't so lucky. For breaching civil service rules by going public with her story, she faced being dismissed from her job.

Prescott's new image as a sexual predator was, however, sealed, as was his link with cocktail sausages. Rumour has it that several deliveries of prime English sausages were made to his offices at the Commons. Whether Prescott accepted them is unknown.

David Mills and Aircraft to Iran
Mark Williams

D avid Mills, the husband of Tessa Jowell, Secretary of State for Culture, Media and Sport, is well known for his dealings with the billionaires Silvio Berlusconi and Bernie Ecclestone, but the exploits that would have really set Nye Bevan and Keir Hardie spinning in their graves were his attempted dealings with Iran.

Aircraft finance is a complicated business, and Mills was not noted for his expertise in that area, so it was perhaps surprising when he was approached in early 2002 by an Iranian businessman, Mohammed Zolanvari, a trader operating in Dubai with strong connections at the heart of the Iranian government, and in particular with former president Rafsanjani. The Rafsanjani family is one of the richest in Iran with wide interests in Kerman province, including the local airline Mahan Air, which had often benefited from preferential treatment over the ailing state airlines, Iran Air and Iran Aseman. The Iranians had agreed to buy several used Airbus aircraft from Turkish Airlines and needed to raise finance for them, although Zolanvari had agreed to underwrite the purchase. In 2002 and 2003, the Iranians raised the required finance in the London banking market and Mills acted as their lawyer in completing the transactions.

Selling aircraft to Iran is fraught with problems, not least because of a US embargo that prevents the sale of aircraft to Iran with more than 10 per cent US manufactured content. Since almost all large modern aircraft have engines or avionics made in the US it was very difficult to avoid the embargo. The aircraft from Turkish Airlines were not caught because the US parts were exported before the date of the embargo in 1995, but following a number of fatal crashes in Iran, the Iranian government ordered airlines to only buy aircraft less than five years old. This was a problem for Mills and his friends, who had been approached by an UK-based Iranian broker who offered them a deal on 12 new and used RJ-146 aircraft from British Aerospace. BAe was not likely to jeopardise its substantial US defence business by exporting embargoed aircraft to Iran, but were keen to sell the last production aircraft before they shut their commercial aviation business. Mills suggested a solution. He would speak to Baroness Symons, the Foreign Office Minister, asking for her help in smoothing the deal with the US authorities. Jowell and Mills were guests at a dinner party at Oxford given by Vernon Bogdanor, professor of politics and government at Brasenose College. Mills sat next to Baroness Symons and talked to her about his problem. Ten days later he wrote to her asking for advice. Symons responded that she had been in touch with the British embassy in Washington and had not had a favourable response, but she was available for further help if required.

Mills initially claimed that Jowell's permanent secretary had been informed, but he later admitted that this was not the case. When contacted later he said: "I have checked. I have not disclosed the fact that I work for an Iranian group because it doesn't infringe on her department at all." Mills also denied that he had been offered further assistance by Symons, but when the *Observer* published Symons' response in January 2005, this was shown to be untrue, and indeed two months later, the Baroness announced her retirement from the Government even though she was only in her early fifties.

Mills' claim that his work did not infringe on his wife's department somehow missed the point. As Secretary of State for Culture, Jowell was one of three ministers who attended regular meetings to approve proposed exports to dubious countries such as Iran. After her husband's involvement with Iran became known, the policy ministerial review of Iranian exports was changed to a review by senior civil servants. The Government claimed this had nothing to do with Mills, but it was a curious change of policy in view of the increased security risks in the region. In 2006 the government disclosed that as a consequence of Mr Mills' business interests, Ms Jowell had been excluded from Cabinet papers and talks on Iran since 2003 – probably the only time that the affairs of a minister's spouse have taken precedence over the affairs of state.

Clearly, Jowell would have been very aware of the restrictions on trading with Iran. All the more curious then when one weekend in February 2003, Mills took three businessmen from Aurigny Air in the Channel Islands to Tehran to put a deal to the Iranians to operate aircraft in and out of Iran from Dubai. At a time when Ms Jowell was urging the country to war with Iraq in support of our US allies, her husband was trying to make a fast buck in the far more dangerous adjacent country by undermining the foreign policy of that very same ally.

In 2003, it was revealed he was involved in an unsuccessful deal for Iranian airline Mahan Air to buy a fleet of BAe 146 aircraft from British Aerospace. He said the sale did not go through and that he was not granted any preferential treatment. However, Foreign Office Minister Baroness Symons gave advice to Mills on the political climate surrounding the project.

Cherie Blair's £1,200-a-Minute Fee

Ellee Seymour

With Labour's popularity sinking to an all-time low since 1992 and Conservatives storming ahead with an eight-point lead, Cherie Blair quite clearly had her priorities set out – cashing in on a lucrative speaking engagement in Dubai to boost her bank account.

Public criticism of the high fees she demands has done nothing to deter her from exploiting her privileged position in pursuit of even greater wealth. In the past she has also been criticised for using her Downing Street flat for business meetings at the taxpayers' expense.

However, on 13th May 2006 she excelled herself by earning £24,000 for a 20-minute lecture – that is £1,200 a minute – to students from the American University of Dubai.

Incredibly, her lecture was held on the same day that Mrs Blair was reported in *The Times* as saying that most of her foreign speaking engagements were unpaid. She insisted that she did not receive fees for talks she made during a recent trip to Pakistan stating quite firmly: "I do these things all the time and I don't get paid for them".

But it transpired that Mrs Blair's Dubai visit had been booked through an American agency for £24,000. On top of that she was given £6,500 first-class flights from Heathrow and £800-a-night luxury five-star suites, bringing the true cost of her visit nearer to £32,000. She was joined by two British protection officers and her agent.

Although the visit was advertised as promoting Cherie Booth QC, she was introduced as somebody with outspoken views who had the ability to multi-task as a wife, mother and professional, a figure worthy of public attention in her own right.

Her brief speech included telling the mainly Arabic audience about the need to promote greater equality and utilise the skills of women. It was never sensational and failed to be outspoken.

But it is not just cashing in on speeches as the Prime Minister's wife that has led to Mrs Blair being accused of abusing her position, she has also been criticised for using her Downing Street flat to hold meetings with clients in her legal capacity as a barrister and QC at the taxpayers' expense.

According to *The Lawyer* magazine, she held some consultations at home as part of her work as an employment law specialist at Matrix Chambers.

The Blairs occupy an extended family flat above Nos 11 and 12 Downing Street, which is paid for by the taxpayer.

It first emerged that Mrs Blair was holding business meetings at No 11 when she was working on the case surrounding the collapsed BCCI bank for her former chambers, 4-5 Gray's Inn Square.

She faced censure from critics who said the property was funded by the taxpayer and should not be used for business purposes.

Mrs Blair was criticised for hosting work meetings in

Downing Street by the Criminal Law Solicitors' Association in August 2000.

Franklin Sinclair, its chairman, said at the time: "You have to ask who is paying for the conference and its administration. She should use her chambers like everyone else."

Mrs Blair has maintained her legal practice despite being the Prime Minister's wife. However, her legal role has brought her into conflict with the Government, particularly over her speciality of employment law and human rights.

Ellee Seymour, www.elleeseymour.blogspot.com

Manchester – so much to answer for.
William Luckman

Manchester Airport PLC's accounts have been known to include a disclaimer to this effect: "We do not make political donations of any sort". Nothing very exciting or controversial there, as plenty of publicly owned and traded companies take the same approach.

However, Manchester Airport is not of a type with BAA – it is owned by a consortium of local authorities in the North West, the vast majority of them historically or currently ruled by the Labour Party, including majority shareholder, Manchester City Council.

As municipal leaders have shown many times in the past, there is plenty of scope for causing mischief without going *ultra vires* or otherwise breaking the law, and for a body that is 'owned by the people of Manchester' to pass money to its ideological soul mates in Westminster might be thought to be a little less than ethical.

However, Manchester Airport Group, which also owns East Midlands Airport, has given the Labour Party some £174,075.00 since 2002. In April 2006, that made it the 26th most generous contributor to the party since 2002.

Although the money was passed over in the form of sponsorships, the Political Parties Elections and Referendums Act 2000 classes any sponsorship of more than £5,000 as a cash donation, and given that any money a political party receives in this way is money it does not have to find elsewhere, that is exactly how it should be treated – money made for the people of Greater Manchester by the company owned by the constituent councils and given to the Labour Party.

This raises a number of points of company law that are perhaps best left to greater experts, although one might ask about the nature of the fiduciary duties owed by directors to shareholders. If whoever cleared the decision to bung money to the Labour Party had not a scintilla of doubt about the wisdom or the ethical issues raised by this, one does have to wonder whether that person has ever read up on corporate governance or even basic company law. Was there the expectation of a quid pro quo, was it a straightforward back scratch for ideological allies, or being *very* charitable, reckoned to be MAG's good deed for the year by way of supporting democracy? Perhaps we will never know. Further to that, every pound given to 'Millbank' was a pound that could have been returned to the shareholders or invested in the business.

Confronted with this action by, of all organisations, the BBC, MAG asked for its money back, and got *some* of it. It would appear that there is some £71,000 that Labour kept and spent on whatever it thought fit. Labour itself attempted to legitimise this by arguing that MAG is a separate legal entity, even though the CEO at the time claimed that the group "is owned by the people of Greater Manchester".

The Croydonian, http://croydonian.blogspot.com

A Weekend Guest

Tom Paine

L et your imagination roam. Picture this. You are 31st richest man in the world's richest country – ranked one place above Rupert Murdoch. You are the greatest American cattle baron, owning more farmland and more stock than any of your fellow citizens. Your personal ranch sits on an estimated 1 billion barrels of crude oil and boasts its own golf course and health spa.

You own or hold shares in about a hundred U.S. corporations, including railways, oil companies, newspapers, radio stations and sports clubs. You are an entertainment mogul, controlling the film rights to the "Narnia" stories by CS Lewis, for example.

One of your sports teams currently employs former England captain David Beckham. You have private boxes at the stadiums where all your teams play. For that matter, you could get tickets and travel to watch any sports team in the world this weekend. Real Madrid? Manchester United? Not a problem. You can afford a box. In fact, you could afford to buy both clubs.

With a personal fortune of almost $8 billion, you are a man with a lot of choices. You are also an educated man. You graduated from your University at the top of your class. You are an art collector. You are also a man of profound religious faith. You have firm moral values and are a devout member of an evangelical church. You personally fund a lobby group that files the majority of "indecency" complaints to America's media watchdog. You also funded a campaign against equal rights for gays and lesbians in your home State. Questioned about your approach to life, you have spoken about "basic beliefs" and "family values". To tell the truth, you are something of a prude.

Are you in this man's skin yet? Excellent. In case you are curious, your name is Phillip. Now, Phil, I have a question for you. What do you want to do this weekend?

$8 billion isn't what it used to be, but it still goes a long way. With that kind of money you could easily afford a trip into Space. Still, that's probably far too immodest for a religious man like you. Maybe you would prefer to go to church with your family? Do some work for your favorite charities? Remember that you are wealthier than some small countries. You can do anything, go anywhere and buy whatever you want.

While you are thinking about it, let me ask you this. With whom you would like to spend your weekend? Your wealth could open many doors. If you chose, you could spend it in the company of some of the most interesting, talented people in the world. Modest as you are about your accomplishments, Phil, I have read that you attribute your success to surrounding yourself with "people who are skilful and bright."

So, given all your options, Phil here is a great idea for you. How would you like to spend the weekend with a fat, uncultured, lecherous slob? How would you like to invite into your family home a foreigner with a history of violence and sexual harassment? He's an elderly English guy with a chip on his shoulder; a class-warrior Socialist who hates people like you with a passion? I should mention that, if you invite him, he would be bringing his freeloading entourage to eat you out of ranch and home.

There is a more serious problem I should mention, Phil. This could be a potential PR disaster. He could make or break one of your UK investments. He is a Government Minister with ultimate responsibility for some project in London; a white elephant of a building in London's

Docklands, apparently. It seems it belongs to one of your companies that is trying to open it as a casino.

So he will need to keep the visit quiet. He won't be making a formal disclosure to Britain's Parliament, as he should. At least, he won't unless the story comes out. You know what journalists are like, Phil. If they get hold of this, they will make out you were up to no good. For a moral guy like you, I know that's a problem. So whatever you do, if he comes by, don't talk to the schmuck about business, OK? That's really important.

So what do you say, Phil? Are you interested? You are? That's great! I'll set it up. What's that, Phil? Sure, I can organize some gifts for him. What's the budget? $20,000? Perfect. That should buy a whole heap of Western stuff for him. I have another idea. When he's had his fill of riding the range in his new cowboy suit, why don't you fly him to him to Los Angeles? You can entertain him to a soccer match in your private box at L.A. Galaxy. OK? Great!

This is really big of you; Phil. I am truly impressed. After all, there's really nothing in it for you. You can't talk about business. That would be wrong. So what are you going to talk about, Phil? I'm guessing he's not very big on art, culture or religion. Maybe you could brush up on British history? Then you can chat to him about – oh, I don't know – "Wilberforce and the abolition of slavery" or something. I'll find you a book.

I have to be honest, Phil. I don't know if I would do this in your place. If I were you, I would rather fly over the Great Wall of China in a helicopter or go fishing on a private yacht. Or maybe I would visit with the Pope in the Vatican or cruise some art galleries to add to my collection. It's really Christian of you to spend time with this guy. He is one of God's less impressive creations. Oh and … Phil? If I were you, I would keep the ladies of your household out of his way. He likes to lift skirts and check out if they are wearing pantyhose or stockings...

…Here he comes now Phil: the ideal weekend companion for a wealthy, cultured, religious businessperson. "John, let me introduce you to my friend Philip Anschutz. Phil, meet John Prescott."

The Last Ditch, www.lastditch.typepad.com

Kicking a Man When He's Dead
Phil Hendren

W hen it comes to fighting, one general rule is that you "never kick a man when he's down". In the case of our illustrious and sleaze-ridden Nu-Labour administration, breaking this rule is not in the least bit uncommon (as many of the preceding pages have shown). However, in May 2006, the rule was taken to a new level as they kicked a man who was not only down, but six feet under too.

Initially only covered as a two inch column filler in the *Evening Standard*'s Londoner's Diary column, it was reported that the Prime Minister's wife, Cherie Blair, along with Alastair Campbell, the former head spinner from Number 10, had signed, for auction at a party political fund-raiser in aid of Chris "underpants" Bryant (see earlier pages for reference), a copy of the Hutton Report.

If ever there was an act that not only showed poor judgement but was the height of bad taste it was this one. After all, this was not just any old report, but was the one into the tragic suicide of a Government scientist. What's more, Alastair Campbell had featured heavily in the report, and to many had played a pivotal role in bringing about the circumstances that led to Dr. David Kelly's death.

As the level-headed, and by now well-versed reader in New Labour sleaze will know, this is exactly the kind of story where you'd expect the rapid news management machine of Downing Street's Communication team to go into overdrive, and yet it didn't happen.

The result was that instead of the spectacular kick in the teeth to the Kelly family being reported heavily by the media, the story remained a diary column entry for another three days. It was not until the *Evening Standard*'s sister paper, the *Mail on Sunday* ran with the tale that the seeds of wider coverage were laid.

On the following Monday morning, the Blogfather (also one of the editors of this book), Iain Dale, gently watered the sprouting shoots of the story by posting it on his blog and asking why no one in the mainstream media had picked up on it. At first he found himself accused of making the story up by his comment makers, but then after a scan of the story was also posted and the day progressed it became all too clear that the story had legs.

Before the end of that Monday, a motion (EDM 2224) had been tabled in Parliament condemning the "appalling bad taste" of the auction, and the "crassly insensitive" act of "seeking to make money, albeit indirectly, through hawking, as a novelty item, an official Government report into the death of a public servant". The motion went on to call on the "Labour Party to apologise for such tasteless and offensive conduct and to donate the money raised to an appropriate charity."

By Tuesday, after Iain Dale had again highlighted the sclerosis of the MSM, the growth in condemnation for such a flagrant act of poor taste had spilled over onto the rolling news channels. The talking heads started appearing saying that Cherie Blair should apologise and then one of those "you couldn't make it up" moments suddenly occurred.

As the media began to bay for the blood of Cherie, everyone who was anyone wanted to appear making comments on news channels and shows about the affair. One such person was Cherie's former aide Fiona Millar. Millar went on to *Sky News* and said that "the right thing [for Cherie] to do is to apologise". Why should this be a "you couldn't make it up" moment? Well... Fiona Millar just happens to be the long-term partner of errrr.... Alastair Campbell. In Millar's eyes, Cherie was utterly wrong to sign the report (correct), her boyfriend however, by omission, was not (incorrect). Tony Blair then found himself questioned about the incident in Parliament and, in an astoundingly glib response, said that he did not "think any offence was intended". As if that made it all all right.

When it comes to sleazy acts, it is arguable that this incident among the many, not the few, is one of the most serious. For it not only showed the sheer arrogance and disdain with which those in the upper echelon of New Labour hold the lives of men driven to suicide, but it also shows the audacity in considering that responsibility for actions is never, in their minds, theirs.

They came into power promising moral clarity and a desire to wipe away the years of "Tory sleaze", and then within seconds repeatedly brushed aside their own sleaze as things we should all tolerate.

Dizzy Thinks http://dizzythinks.net

Gord-Balls Hash
Damon Lambert

Sorry to interrupt you from salacious scandals but it's time to talk numbers. Here's Ed and Gordon's recipe for cooking the books.

First, choose your meal carefully. For starters, make the Sustainable Investment Rule that public sector net debt must not be more than 40% of GDP in each year of the economic cycle. For main course, bake the Golden Rule that you will borrow only to invest and not to fund current spending.

Make sure that you are the only chef. The last thing you want is some independent arbitrator butting in and telling you that you have messed up. Be your own judge of your own cooking.

Don't put all the ingredients in. If you ate all the Pension Fund tax credits before you finished your first Budget, then you can miss the public sector pension deficit off the menu. Whilst your own statisticians may estimate the hole to be £530 billion, top actuaries Watson Wyatt may have distrusted your numbers and done their own calculations, based upon, and I use their phrase "a realistic basis". They came up with £960 billion hole. That's 73.5% of 2006-07 GDP, and in itself almost double the debt you need for the Sustainable Investment Rule, so leave that off the table or voters appetites might collapse.

Many would be tempted to use tools such as ordinary gilts and bonds, readily available at low interest rates for any UK government to borrow with. However, expensive PFI projects make a more than tasty substitute for many a large business to profit from. Don't serve PFI immediately, it's best left off-balance sheet for several years (current temperature is £155 billion (12% of GDP)).

Overcook the public sector part of the dish but don't forget to trim UK competitiveness on a regular basis. Let the yeast cause the taxcode to rise until it's at least double the size of when you first got it. Leave the tax credit mess, that can be cleaned up later.

When the dish is in the oven then watch the timing. If the 7 year recipe does not look like it will work for the Golden Rule then don't be afraid to move the economic cycle to 12 years. If that does not work, then turn it down to 10 years. Great thing about this dish, is that you can make these changes eight years after the event and fool yourself that no-one will notice. When moving onto the next economic cycle don't tell anyone, as it might mean you will get away with the fact that you will miss it by an estimated £66 billion. Keep the ingredients flexible, you might need to reclassify road spending as capital as time progresses.

Serve in March each year in a well-greased monologue. Drizzle with snot and garnish with a generous amount of spin.

Taxcutter, http://thetaxcutter.blogspot.com

Tony Blair and Christmas 2006
Ellee Seymour

Tony Blair's last Christmas holiday fling as Prime Minister caused controversy for more than one reason. He had been hoping to keep his plans for some winter sun with his family quiet. But unfortunately for him, their jet made a dramatic landing at Miami when it overshot the runway, sending hordes of journalists rushing to the scene.

The duration of his stay as a guest of former Bee Gees singer Robin Gibb remained stormy too, with constant headlines in the UK accusing him of soaking up another freebie – as well as the Florida sun.

Yet again, the Blairs were accused of making the most of their position by capitalising on the hospitality of celebrities, of the rich and famous. The Gibbs' opulent £5.8 million mansion is in one of Miami's "millionaires rows". It has its own swimming pool and boat dock, along with 10-bedrooms and nine-bathrooms, and is surrounded by a swarm of security guards. Neighbours include Robin's brother Maurice, as well as singer Ricky Martin and Hollywood star Matt Damon.

While Blair was most likely strumming on his guitar with his music idol, journalists back home remained unconvinced about the funding for this trip, questioning whether the Blairs were really paying their own way as claimed. However, Robin's wife Dwina said the couple had not for asked or accepted money from the Blairs.

Blair's other generous hosts have included Cliff Richard who loaned his Caribbean villa, Geoffrey Robinson and his 10-acre Tuscan estate, Prince Girolamo Strozzi's 16th century Tuscan palace, and Silvio Berlusconi's 73-room Sardinian estate.

The situation worsened when Blair faced claims of a conflict of interest because Robin Gibb had been lobbying the Government to change its policy towards pop musicians. The Gibb brothers have been leading a campaign by the British Academy of Composers & Songwriters which urged the Government to tighten copyright protection for artists. This clearly demonstrated a lack of judgement, and left a sour note, showing Blair is clearly not tuned in.

Chris Grayling, Shadow Transport Minister, put it succinctly when he said:

"Another year, another celebrity holiday and yet more questions about Tony Blair's judgement. The trouble is that he doesn't seem to realise that when he does things like this it just causes more damage to the reputation of politicians as a whole".

No wonder Gordon Brown has already stated he plans to distance himself from the celebrity culture.

Tony's going on a 'Summer Holiday', no more working for a week or two.......

Ellee Seymour, www.elleeseymour.com

We're All Going on a Summer Holiday
UK Paul

Tony Blair might usually have stayed at that dodgy Berlusconi bloke's place but, given his reputation, you can imagine what the press would have been saying, so how about staying at the Peter Pan of pop's gaff in Barbados instead? Surely that would be seen as above any accusations of sleaze or of supporting certain Italian megalomaniacs?

Apparently Cliff lent Blair the use of house in Barbados because of how "dwindled and haggard" he looked after the Iraq war, nothing to how the Iraqi people look after the botched occupation, but that's by the by. What some may have missed, however, is that Cliff has been banging on about extending copyright terms for ages. At the moment, recorded works become public domain after 50 years and performers no longer receive royalties but Cliff and some other stars of a certain vintage want this to become 75 years or so. Beats saving for a pension any day.

On the surface it sounds laudable – help poor elderly musicians who have fallen on hard times and all that, except that those who were the jobbing musicians often got a one off sum and no royalties, so no pay-day for them. Those who would benefit are those who could still sell a lot of discs, as in those who are pretty much loaded anyway.

On top of this there is a whole industry of public domain labels that release recordings out of copyright (and of small independent record shops that profit from selling them). Often these are 'labour of love' and rare recordings that would otherwise disappear. Our recorded heritage is in danger of looking "dwindled and haggard" if we keep it in the hands of copyright owners beyond the current time. Record companies abandon all but a very small percentage of their catalogue and much may disappear unsaved. Writers do get paid royalties for up to 70 years by the way so, if Cliff had got his finger out and written his songs he wouldn't be moaning so much.

Amazingly (or not), the issue of copyright extension was subsequently presented to ministers as a matter of importance but, thankfully, an official review of the matter told them to stick the idea where the sun don't shine brightly.

That should, of course, be that but, depressingly, a cross party committee of MPs has now resurrected the idea and we can expect it to rumble on and on. In the meantime Cliff's house-lending largesse has been joined by that of Robin Gibb of the Bee Gees, Now if this group of well off stars were to use their access to the highest level of government for their own personal ends that really would be a 'Tragedy'.

The Trade Union 'Modernisation' Fund
Remittance Man

L ike a lot of the sleaze allegations surrounding this government, the story of the Trade Union Modernisation Fund revolves around money. More specifically, the money needed to keep the increasingly expensive Labour Party machine in operation and to fund its election campaigns. Those Cherie Blair haircuts don't come cheap, after all.

And despite his best efforts to distance the party from the old left, Tony Blair finds himself still beholden to the trade unions for a massive amount of cash each year. From the Electoral Commission website it is possible to see that combined affiliation fees and donations from trades unions amounted to 55% of the Labour Party's income in 2003 and 62% in 2004.

All this at a time when the unions themselves were losing members and hence funds, with little or no reduction in their long term commitments to things like pensions – which were probably raided by Mr Brown just like everyone else's. Also the new generation of union leaders was less appreciative of Tony's Third Way; they much prefer the idea of the Old Way.

So faced with a growing dependence upon money from an increasingly cash-strapped and bolshie source, Tony had to come up with a plan. That's when someone thought of a stunningly simple wheeze: Get the unions to bankroll the party (especially the 2005 general election campaign) in return for a promise of taxpayer money over the next few years.

Of course this had to be dressed up a bit so the Trade Union Modernisation Fund was born. Ostensibly this is supposed to assist trade unions "train representatives, introduce new technology, review their management and structures" and, despite a clause in the legislation banning the use of modernisation funds for recruitment, "encourage under represented groups such as young people to join unions". Now I don't know about you, but I would have thought that trade unions should be setting up websites and teaching shop stewards how to use e-mail out of their own pockets; it's what everybody else does after all.

The original budget was for £5–10 million spread over several years with expenditure starting in fiscal year 2006-7. Of course like most government estimates the chance this fund will stay within these rather airy budget parameters or even die in a few years is highly unlikely. The unions certainly view its existence as a semi-permanent feature; in a 2005 document they list abolition of the fund as one of the most damaging things a new Conservative government could do.

Whether the funds are being directed to non-approved activities or not is only likely to be revealed by the police investigation (yes another one) launched in 2006. But even if the money is being used on the "right" things, as an example of one branch of the left scratching another's back at taxpayers expense, this is hard to beat.

The Remittance Man http://remittanceman.blogspot.com

David Blunkett —
A very socialist capitalist
Gregor Hopkins

David Blunkett our former Home Secretary, former Work and Pensions Secretary, former die-hard socialist, former enemy of Thatcherism, former, to some anyway, role model, is by all accounts quite an interesting fellow.

A philanderer and serial despoiler of the ministerial code, he was twice kicked out of Cabinet level positions for conduct quite unbecoming a minister, while at the same time racking up quite a lucrative series of interests to bolster not only his own bank account, but to remain solvent in the face of a rapidly expanding "network of friends" to put it succinctly.

The long and short of it is that the ex leader of what is fondly remembered as the 'Socialist Republic of South Yorkshire' (probably less fondly by those who lived there at the time) is now a dyed in the wool free marketeer, and with knobs on! He has in fact completely contradicted himself. Less a realignment of views, more a full conversion with baptism included!

Whilst Home Secretary he submerged himself within a neo-con persona that would have elicited cries of fascist had it been anyone else. His authoritarian bent is not the only thing that animates us big book bloggers. Whilst not forgetting his shares in DNA Biosciences, the very mention of which is a sure-fire faux pas at Labour party dinner parties everywhere, his diary deals (approx £280,000 in rights and payments), serialisations (the *Grauniad* and the *Daily Mail* £100,001-£105,000), speaking engagements (approx £30,000) and even newspaper columns (approx £150,000 2005-7 for *The Sun*). All rake in a very tidy sum for someone seemingly opposed to the excesses of capitalism. This is of course all noted tidily, and seemingly without embarrassment in the Register of Members' Interests.

My last criticism and perhaps the sleaziest of Blunkett's many infamies is an almost poetic combination of his two major flaws. I refer of course to Blunkett's new job, advising the Texan security firm Entrust which is bidding to run our next £20 Billion IT debacle, the ID cards scheme! In this new venture he has managed to combine both his money grabbing and authoritarian instincts into one super job. A stiff rebuttal to all who say Blair's Britain is a less socially mobile place.

The Blog http://gregor.org.uk

Charge it to the Party Faithful
Damon Lambert

You might be thinking that New Labour sneered at pensioners, current and future, as a generic group. In fact, it selected its very own party staff for the very biggest of kickings. Based on Labour's most recent published Financial Statements, its own Staff Pension Fund has a big black hole of £6.3 million. Given the organisation has total net liabilities of £27 million this isn't going to get filled in a hurry. Basically, the Labour Party is funding itself via a large loan from its staff's Pension Fund, a loan on which, despite the very low credit rating of the borrower, no interest is necessarily due. And to add insult to injury, rumour has it that the Labour Party Staff Pension Fund wasn't even offered a lordship for its efforts. Will the problem get solved? Well, given that Jack Dromey, the Labour Party Treasurer did not realise that the organisation whose finances he manages had £18 million of loans (I'm not saying I don't believe Mr Harriet Harman but if I was heavily overdrawn and then suddenly got a bank statement saying I was £18 million up on what I was expecting, plus I was subject to the Electoral Reform Commission's strict rules on donations from, then I'd find out very quickly where that money came from), let's not count on him spotting this big problem too quickly either.

So who runs the risk that there just won't be enough funds in the pot to keep the Labour Party's staff with income in retirement, income they are clearly due under law? Well it's certainly not Labour MPs. Their Pension Funds are generously underwritten by the taxpayer. Normally Labour, would like any other organisation in financial trouble, have to either increase membership subscriptions to cover the hole and/or cut costs. Yet the government does seem increasingly fond on getting taxpayers to fund political parties . . .

Taxcutter http://thetaxcutter.blogspot.com

Burying Bad News ... Again

Daniel Harvey

When Jo Moore sent her now infamous e-mail on September 11th 2001, no-one thought that the Government would be accused of doing the same again, or in such style as they did on 14th December 2006.

Recent news focussed on events in Ipswich where 5 prostitutes had been strangled, and where Police were still searching for the murderer. It would also be the day on which Lord Stevens would announce the findings of his report into the deaths of Diana Princess of Wales, and Dodi Fayed. Labour wouldn't use this as an opportunity to try and sneak out some 'bad news' would they? Of course they would.

That morning, the Prime Minister's official spokesman gave no indication that the Prime Minister would be interviewed by the police investigating the sale of Honours in return for Loans to the Labour Party, but it later became clear that the Prime Minister had been interviewed by the police, and that the interview took place between the end of the weekly cabinet meeting and the Prime Minister leaving to attend a meeting of the European Council in Brussels.

Or if that wasn't enough bad news to bury, how about the Attorney General announcing that the Serious Fraud Office had dropped a corruption probe into a defence deal with Saudi Arabia, after warnings it could damage national security. Lord Goldsmith said the SFO was "discontinuing" its investigation into Britain's biggest defence company, BAE Systems, adding that both Mr Blair and Defence Secretary Des Browne had argued that carrying on the investigation would harm intelligence and diplomatic co-operation with Saudi Arabia.

Not convinced?

How about the announcement that 2,500 Post Offices would be closed?

The Prime Ministers official spokesman emphasised that there was no deliberate plan to "bury bad news" by holding the interview on the same day Lord Stevens released his report into the death of Princess Diana. "Categorically there was no linkage to other events," he said, and that the Prime Minister had chosen the day of the interview.

Philip Webster, Political Editor of *The Times*, said that "The obvious charge is that Downing Street deliberately timed it to coincide with a huge news day – with the Ipswich serial killer, the Diana report and the announcement on the closure of post offices. Mr Blair couldn't have foreseen the Ipswich story but the other two could have been foreseen."

And as Iain Dale put it on his blog – "Astonishingly Sky have moved away from Ipswich and are staying with Lord Stevens. So far they have spent twenty seconds on the Post Office closures. Number Ten will be pleased."

And if you thought it would stop then, how about Tony Blair making the announcement that he would be standing down as Prime Minister at the same time as the Bank of England announced the latest increase in Interest Rates.

Some things never change.

The Tools to do the Job
James Cleverly

Sleaze comes in many forms, some trivial and amusing, some significant and deeply serious. The cynical and deceitful way that Labour has treated the troops in Afghanistan falls squarely into the second category.

Having been assured by the then Defence Secretary, John Reid, that the mission in Helmand province could be completed without a shot being fired 16 Air Assault Brigade was sent off to some of the most intense fighting since the Falklands. They were short of troops, short of equipment, short of ammunition and short of support from their own government. Unsurprisingly their casualties and fatalities were heavy. Things didn't improve during the "winter lull" when the Royal Marine Commandos took over.

The plight of the armed forces had been the dog that didn't bark for a number of elections and Labour clearly thought that it was an issue that they could conveniently sweep under the carpet. How wrong they were.

The rate of military losses crept into the public consciousness and was reinforced by the unprecedented criticism of the government by senior members of the Army. Blair had to be seen to do something.

In October 2006 Blair promised military commanders that they could have whatever they needed to get the job done. What military commanders asked for were more helicopters and more troops. What they got was the financial obstacle that is Gordon Brown.

No increase in helicopter procurement has happened meaning the promise of more air mobility was a hollow one. And when the commander of 12 Mechanised Brigade asked to have an extra battalion added to their numbers for the deployment to Afghanistan he was told "NO"! The MOD finally relented and added the battalion half way through the pre-deployment training program.

In training soldiers are told over and over again that accuracy of information is key. Decisions are made based on the information they provide, if they provide inaccurate information planners make inappropriate decisions and lives are lost.

British military planning has been hampered at so many levels by Labour's spin, media obsession and headlines over substance attitude. Labour have promised much and failed to deliver in so many areas that it seems almost stupid to hope that they would do any different in Afghanistan.

The difference is that in Afghanistan their inability to tell the truth has cost lives.

James Cleverly http://jamescleverly.blogspot.com

A Fair Day's Pay?
Dominic Fisher

Exploitation of British media workers is rife, but you wouldn't expect it from the Labour Party, would you? Well, would you?

For someone trying to break into the media industry, an opportunity to work with Labour's media team on video productions for their party conference sounded attractive. At least, that's what student Danny Dewsbury thought in August 2006 when he took a work experience role with the Labour Party in the lead up to Labour 2006 Party Conference in Manchester. At that time, Danny was living on an office floor struggling with a five figure student debt. By taking this marvellous opportunity to gain new skills working for the Labour Party, he sacrificed paid work.

To his surprise, instead of work experience, Danny found that he was charged with full responsibility to produce a series of videos of Cabinet Ministers to be used at the Labour Party conference. Indeed, nobody was on hand to teach him anything about the media and Danny also had to supply film equipment and pay for travel to locations in Salford, Hull and London out of his own pocket. When Danny pointed out to Emmet Regan (PA to Labour Party Chairman Hazel Blears) that this was in fact real work and he should get paid, he was firmly rebuffed. A call to the government's National Minimum Wage helpline confirmed Danny's suspicion that due to legislation enacted under Blair's watch, the Labour Party could not legally classify him as a volunteer and that he was entitled to the minimum wage. His rogue employers in the Labour Party didn't see things that way.

The press picked up on the story which was featured on TV and in the national print media during the Conference, but Labour still wouldn't even pay the work expenses Danny had incurred never mind a fair day's wage for a fair day's work. So in November 2006, a cross-party group of bloggers angered by this hypocritical exploitation, threatened to step in to meet Labour's financial obligation to pay the minimum wage for Danny's work. This high profile campaign embarrassed Labour and finally set the wheels in motion for Danny to get paid.

The story has a final twist. Based on video footage assembled from his time working for Labour, Danny made a short film which provides a stark warning to aspiring media professionals about employer exploitation. "Slave Labour" beat 90 other films to sweep the board at the National Student Film Festival awards.

Prague Tory http://praguetory.blogspot.com

Campbell's Crocodile Tears
Paul Linford

It is no great secret either within the political blogosphere or within my former stamping ground, the Lobby, that I do not have a huge amount of time for Alastair Campbell. I imagine the feeling is fairly mutual.

By and large, I agree with the assessment of the former Tory leader Michael Howard, as memorably expressed in a *Newsnight* discussion panel on the night of Tony Blair's resignation, that it was Campbell who bore the greatest responsibility for the collapse of public trust in politics that occurred under New Labour.

There is one aspect of Alastair's story, though, that has always commanded a certain amount of respect from his journalistic peers, namely the way in which he overcame serious mental health problems in his late 20s before going on to have a highly effective, if controversial career in government.

So it was no great surprise when, in the autumn of 2006, the *Independent on Sunday* chose to use an interview with Campbell as the centrepiece of a special edition highlighting the issue of mental health.

I don't doubt for a moment that Campbell's primary intention in carrying out this interview was to help draw attention to the issue, in the hope that his story might be seen as an inspiration to others. But ever the spin doctor, he could not resist the temptation to present a completely disingenuous and self-serving account of the David Kelly affair.

Dr Kelly was, of course, the Ministry of Defence weapons expert who took his own life in July 2003 after being unmasked by Government officials as the source of a controversial BBC report alleging that the dossier on Iraqi weapons of mass destruction had been "sexed up."

In the IoS interview, Campbell admitted that the death of Dr Kelly was his "worst day" – and how his earlier experience of a crippling breakdown in his 20s helped him to cope.

He said: "It [the Hutton saga] was one of those episodes where things spiralled out of control... I felt completely confident in relation to the facts but during the whole period it was a nightmare. And you are thinking, 'There's this guy for whom it's been such a nightmare he's killed himself'."

Now as I wrote on my blog at the time, this almost makes it sound like they were all in it together, that Campbell, like Kelly, was the random victim of a process over which none of them, least of all the spin doctor himself, had any control. The facts, as related in Campbell's evidence to the Hutton Inquiry and in his own diaries, are rather different.

Far from having sympathy for the plight of the former weapons inspector, Campbell wanted his name out in the public domain because, as he so poetically put it, it would "fuck Gilligan" – as in Andrew Gilligan, author of the BBC story in question.

As well as that one infamous phrase, the Campbell

diaries also reveal that "GH (Defence Secretary Geoff Hoon) and I both wanted to get the source up but TB was nervous about it," and that he and Hoon "felt we should get it out through the papers then have a line to respond."

In other words, Campbell tried his damnedest to ensure Dr Kelly's exposure, and despite being initially overruled by Tony Blair, in the end he got his way.

In his IoS interview, Campbell described his original breakdown as having been brought on by work, drink and pressure at a time when he was in a job for which he was psychologically unsuited.

Was it not richly ironic that someone who displayed such apparent self-knowledge about what drove him to a "psychotic" breakdown at the age of 28 could fail to show the slightest understanding of his own pivotal role in a tragedy in which someone else was ultimately driven to take his own life?

As the late, great Hugo Young memorably put it in 2003, the death of Dr Kelly was a consequence of "the dynamic that is unleashed when the Prime Minister's sainted reputation becomes the core value his country has to defend."

It was Campbell who unleashed that dynamic by launching his war with the BBC and then pursuing it with apparent disregard for any human consequences. And however many crocodile tears he may shed about it now, it was Campbell who was thus at least indirectly to blame for Dr Kelly's death.

Paul Linford http://paullinford.blogspot.com

Cherie's Gold Rush
Emdad Rahman

June 27th may be the day that the door to untold wealth and glamour are flung open as warmonger and part time Prime Minister Blair takes leave of office to pursue the most lucrative of career, for has been politicians, addressing toffs at after dinner events.

After all Mr Blair can take the scenic route with confidence, with no fear of the future as Cherie "I'm not cashing in on my husband's position" Blair, has already ventured down the seldom trodden path to untold riches.

Sulphur Springs was the venue when our Cherie kick started a lucrative Stateside lecture tour in July 2006, all after all with securing a multi million Connaught Square town house mortgage secured someone had to wear the trousers.

With the web domain, cherieblair.org.uk having been registered, Cherie, very much a part-time judge, struck a cash bonanza, a money churning speaking tour with an organisation that has representation from the likes of Hollywood legends Goldie Hawn and Shirley Maclaine. It seems that Cherie has forever provoked criticism for her over the top fondness of the 'good' things in life. Cherie's legendary partiality towards complimentary has seen the likes of Sir Cliff Richard and Bee Gee Robin Gibb offer freebie jaunts for the Blair clan.

During the tour, "the First Lady of Downing Street",

bizarrely marketed as; "Cherie Booth QC, human rights lawyer, wife of Tony Blair", earned in the region of £100,000 for committing to three speaking engagements.

The question is, did serial juggler Cherie, co-Author of *The Goldfish Bowl*, and who once melted the nation after carping on about the fact that it was very difficult juggling all the balls in the air, fall foul of the ministerial code stating that ministers are themselves accountable to make certain there is no conflict of interest between their profession and any pecuniary interests of their kin?

The humorous Scouser, who once asked a wheel-chair-bound comedian if he was a stand-up was similarly criticised in 2005 after it became apparent that a children's charity fundraising dinner she spoke at received less than 10%, with Cherie pocketing a whopping $38,000.

All of which points to a very golden future. He may be responsible for a lot of the turmoil we witness on our TV screens, but thanks to a media savvy face, spin, Cherie's extra earners and the taste of things to come, it's safe to presuppose that the Blair's will never go hungry again.

All in a Day's Work www.emdad.neemit.net

The Tale of Two Prescotts
William Burstow

In March 2005 Johnathan Prescott, (Fresh from establishing his own property company, Estate Partnerships, with Richard Carlowe) attended the MIPIM property conference in Cannes. It signalled his grand entrance as a big player of the lucrative British property market. It was also attended by his father, the Deputy Prime Minister, and at the time, the minister in charge of housing development.

In August 2006 the media revealed all with details of secret meetings in grace-and-favour residences, attending daddy's local parliamentary events and property deals, negotiated by Lil' John, on places such as Eaglescliffe Logistics Centre, potentially prime property for government housing plans, all of which could have been interpreted as a clear conflict of interest on the part of the Deputy Prime Minster.

In 2001, contractors involved in overhauling a property in South west London allegedly met Lil' John in Admiralty House, the DPM's grace and favour residence in London. Lil' John admits to this, but stated it was not a business meeting, merely a chance to 'show them around' the building. This version of events is disputed in a signed statement provided by one of those present who claims it was in fact a business meeting over the property.

One of the contractors claimed Lil' John also

approached him to see if he and his partner wanted to work for him. They agreed, so in early July 2001 Lil' John invited them down to London. The contractor claims they parked in an official government car park off Whitehall before being led into Admiralty House where they "stayed there for an hour or two and spent most of that time talking about money." However Lil' John disputes this and states that after a "few beers" he invited them in to look around. And that isn't all.

From August 2005 Estate Partnerships had been negotiating on Eaglescliffe. While this was happening Lil' John was involved in talks with Tees Valley Regeneration, the government quango set up to fund redevelopment projects and the previous owners of Eaglescliffe. They had made representations to a government enquiry, which had been established by the Deputy Prime Minster, to draw up development plans for the north east. Their submission states:

"In planning and policy terms the redevelopment of the Eaglescliffe Logistics Centre will represent a classic previously developed windfall opportunity site . . . It terms of the potential housing test it scores highly."

The proposal for the 112-acre site involved 600 new homes being built on the land, 600 new homes which would most likely be part of Big John's proposed housing explosion.

While both Prescotts have denied any conflict, when asked, David Taylor, a former adviser to the DPM, hinted that their interests and paths have crossed in the past. "It is quite possible (that John Prescott has ruled on developments involving his son)," He said. "A lot of planning decisions involving Johnathan could have gone to his department." And the evidence continues to point to a conflict of interest.

Lil' John invited Johnny Gallagher, the man who purchased the Eaglescliffe site, to a parliamentary reception at Parliament hosted by Big John in November of 2005, while they were in negotiations over the Eaglescliffe site. And finally, you wonder what really was Lil' John's role in Estate Partnerships when one property executive has said "you have to ask what value Prescott, who puts in none of his own money, is bringing to the whole deal. The profit is entirely dependent on the planning permission."

http://a-young-conservative.blogspot.com

Lord Sainsbury's Conflict of Interest
Chris Mounsey

Former Science Minister and supermarket billionaire, Lord Sainsbury, has never been a stranger to controversy, facing down criticism for his involvement in GM crops – and alleged conflict of interest in relevent Cabinet decisions – from a number of eco-groups in 2004.

The noble peer is the biggest individual donor to New Labour, having given some £14 million since 1998 and £16m since Tony Blair became leader. Indeed, he narrowly avoided being censured under the ministerial code when he failed to disclose a £2 million loan in April 2006 – he maintained that he had confused it with a declared donation.

As the Loans for Peerages investigation was seriously getting underway, in November 2006, Lord Sainsbury resigned. He had been interviewed as a witness but denied any wrong-doing.

Lord Sainsbury pointed out that he was made a peer "eight or nine years ago" and that although he had made loans and donations to the party, he was "not a fundraiser for the party."

Neither argument is particularly valid since, for all we know, New Labour may well have been taking cash in return for honours since the very beginning, and whether Lord Sainsbury was a fundraiser for the party is surely slightly irrelevant.

However, the peer made every effort to make it absolutely clear that he was resigning to devote himself to his assorted charitable works and other interests and that, after eight years in the job, he had "achieved most of what [he] wanted to achieve."

What it is that Sainsbury has actually achieved is open to debate; this country is not exactly known to be on the cutting edge of scientific achievement in many fields. And, of course, the state of general scientific qualifications in our state schools is best described as 'dismal'. This is due, in no small part, to the propensity, presided over by New Labour, for taking the General Combined Sciences GCSE in preference to the individual disciplines.

But perhaps Lord Sainsbury's achievements will become clear over the coming decades...

Whether the cash for honours scandal had anything to do with Lord Sainsbury's resignation is entirely a matter for the noble peer's own conscience. However, despite Labour sources maintaining that Sainsbury's resignation had been "talked about for quite a long time", the perceived abruptness of his retirement might well have given some pause for thought.

And for many that thought was: is yet another rat leaving the sinking ship?

Devil's Kitchen http://devilskitchen.me.uk

Keeping BAe Out of Arms' Way
Chris Wales

O ver the last 10 years the British public has witnessed many New Labour U-turns; notably, Tony Blair's promise not to give up the rebate and subsequently trading it in for vague French promises; pledging "full support" to ministers before sacking them; and the infamous "we have no plans to raise tax" mantra. So it really should have come as no surprise when the "whiter than white" government was perfectly happy to halt a criminal investigation over bribes to Saudi Arabia when it began to unearth embarrassing truths that the government would rather keep hidden.

Since 1985, a series of large arms sales from Britain to Saudi Arabia have been among British Aerospace's (now BAe's) most lucrative contracts. Named *Al Yamamah* (ironically, Arabic for "the dove"), allegations began to surface in 2001 that these deals took place only on the back of substantial bribes to the Saudi Royal Family. The ideal trading partners, the Saudi establishment is an honest and upright group of rulers whose administration has seen an estimated £400 billion go accidentally missing from their country's public purse.

These allegations took the form of a letter from a BAe employee to the Ministry of Defence outlining the evidence. The letter unexpectedly disappeared for two years and finally reappeared in *The Guardian*, whereupon

24 hours later the Serious Fraud Office took note and began to investigate the claim.

In a U-turn that would do every New Labour spin doctor proud, BAe proudly trumpeted their full co-operation and that they "believe[d] that it would put these matters to rest once and for all", before promptly refusing to comply with compulsory production notices issued for the specifics of its offshore payments to the Middle East. Not to be outdone, New Labour luvvie Patricia Hewitt, serving Trade Secretary, marched into the Commons with a bold face of bewilderment as it emerged that her department had authorised a £1 billion insurance policy to BAe and then concealed it from Parliament in their annual report.

Desperate to avoid upsetting one of America's favourite 'partners' in the War on Terror (ergo, one of Britain's favourite partners), the National Audit Office refused to publish a report on the Al Yamamah contract, making it the first NAO report not to be released, even to criminal investigators. This would presumably make it even more vital to national security than the financial breakdowns for spending on the MI5 and MI6 headquarters, which are freely available.

The Saudis did not take too kindly to open public scrutiny over the deals, particularly when it was made clear in November 2006 that the investigation could continue for a further two years whilst Swiss bank accounts were examined. As threats were bandied around including the severing of diplomatic ties; taking business to France and dropping the latest $6 billion Eurofighter deal, the numbers of threatened job losses began to appear throughout the press.

Enter everyone's favourite Attorney General Lord Goldsmith to valiantly save the day. He warmly invited the investigation team to his office with boxes of all the evidence that had been carefully and painstakingly collected over two years. Unfortunately for the investigators, the Commons and any British citizen wishing to exercise his or her right to see the application of law, he chose to throw his not-so-insubstantial weight behind the case for the 'gravy train' rather than for the prosecution.

In one fell swoop, he announced that it "would not be in the public interest" (apparently, now identical to the government interest) to pursue the investigation, just in time for Tony to jet off to the Middle East and exchange smiles with local dignitaries. Yet again, an inconvenient truth swept under the carpet. Another dismal low for New Labour, cemented only by the public approval of noted perjurer Jonathan Aitken, who applauded the cover-up with typical aplomb.

Too Many Special Advisers
Martin Curtis

The role of a special adviser is to provide the political perspective to a Minister, to do the work within Government that our once independent Civil Servants are not supposed to do.

When Tony Blair came to office there were just thirty-four Special Advisers across the whole of Government. After the coronation of New Labour the number of SpAds rose dramatically, reaching a peak of eighty-four. Of course there was lots of concern about this and about their conduct under New Labour so a report published by the Neill Committee on Standards in Public Life led to the creation of a code of conduct for SpAds, but in true sleazy New Labour fashion, the final decision on whether a Special Adviser's conduct is a sufficient breach of the code was left to the judgement of the person with most interest in retaining them, the employing Minister. The Neill Committee also called for caps on their numbers, but this did not fit in with the Government's desire to politicise the Civil Service so, of course, they rejected the idea.

SpAds have been a significant contributor to the tarnishing of British politics since 1997; the biggest proponent is of course Alastair Campbell, who developed a reputation for bullying and harassing those in the media who dared to disagree with Government policy.

He was also in the middle of a number of scandals. In particular he was accused of being directly responsible for 'sexing up' the alleged 'dodgy dossier' that contributed to the decision to go to war in Iraq.

Another infamous SpAd was Jo Moore, who on the day of the horrific events of 9/11, put out an email suggesting that it was a good day to bury bad news. Of course her boss, then Transport Minister Stephen Byers, didn't think this was a sackable offence and allowed her to continue after issuing an apology, but eventually she was forced to resign after a prolonged and bitter media gossiping campaign.

The Code of Conduct specifically forbids using Government funded SpAds to carry out party political work. This has created something of a problem for the SpAds of those Shadow Cabinet Members who also happen to be Labour Deputy Leadership contenders. A number of them have been accused of acting in direct contravention of the code by actively campaigning for their bosses, in particular by Guido Fawkes (www.order-order.com) through his Shop-a-SpAd campaign.

Of course, when something has the whiff of scandal and sleaze around it you would expect organisations to be wary about making use of those involved. Not New Labour. They continue to use the position of SpAd as a stepping stone to a safe Labour seat and rapid promotion to Ministerial ranks.

Spin Blog www.spinblog.co.uk

The NHS Traffic Lights
Sam Coates

National media coverage gets a red traffic light, regional press an amber light, and if its just local press then that's a green light for go. This was Labour's heat map of the 77 NHS trusts which would cause them the most trouble in the event of cuts or closure. Drawn up with advice from Strategic Health Authorities, it was an impressive database that even predicted the season of the year in which local controversies would likely break.

This was all kick-back from a plan to treat more patients at a community level and focus specialist treatment in regional centres of excellence. It started going murky when this meant choosing which hospitals to close, as a Freedom of Information request from Shadow Health Secretary Andrew Lansley revealed in November 2006.

Activist groups such as Health Emergency, Keep Our NHS Public, and Community Hospitals Acting Nationally Together, in conjunction with the TUC, were already causing Labour MPs a headache in marginal constituencies so the beloved Health Secretary Patricia Hewitt (herself facing a threat to her small majority from a "save the local hospital" candidate similar to Wyre Forest's Richard Taylor) asked civil servants to analyse the electoral danger areas. She then met with Party Chairman Hazel Blears and some Downing Street officials in July to discuss the distribution of the map to senior Labour figures.

The Conservatives didn't get all that they wanted in the FOI request as apparently there were not minutes or agenda for this meeting, and the Health Department refused to release details of discussions between its top officials.

The trusts highlighted included those in the constituencies of Labour's Laura Moffat (majority of 37), Joan Ryan (1,920), Sadiq Khan (5,381) and Barry Gardiner (5,461).

The British Medical Association, political parties, and numerous others were quick to express outrage that these decisions were being made on anything other than clinical criteria.

The consciences of Labour SpAds were probably salved by a belief that putting the Party's need before some patients was a necessary means to the end of another term of Labour government. Problem is, this is the kind of thing the government has become known for. That Labour voting areas have had a highly disproportionate amount of government investment, making it hard for Conservative councils to both pick up the slack and cut taxes, is well documented.

With this self-serving attitude pervading all levels of government, it's no wonder the good British people are more cynical about their rulers than they have been for generations.

ConservativeHome www.conservativehome.com

Breaking the Law:
Gordon Brown's Smith Institute
and Politically Partisan Activity
Guido Fawkes

The Smith Institute is being formally investigated by the Charity Commission for political activity in breach of the Charities Act. Wilf Stevenson, Director of the Smith Institute, claims that "the Smith Institute has never had and does not currently have a direct relationship with Gordon Brown."

The Treasury's pollster Deborah Mattinson of Opinion Leader Research is on the board of the Smith Institute. OLR's polls are notoriously favourable to Gordon Brown. OLR do free polling for the Smith Institute.

In March 2007 Margaret Beckett gave a speech to an assembled audience at No. 11 Downing Street which included Gordon Brown, his long time financial backer and Smith Institute trustee, Lord Haskel. In the speech she praised Gordon to the skies, lauding his record in office saying "..if, as I certainly hope we do, we have the architect of that amazing record, Gordon Brown, as our next Labour Prime Minister".

In January 2007 Wilf Stevenson, Gordon Brown's best friend, emailed left-of-centre think tanks and HM Treasury figures asking them for policy ideas for Gordon Brown's administration. Wilf later claimed it was sent in "a personal capacity". It obviously demonstrated that the Smith Institute was intimately involved in policy formulation for Gordon Brown.

In March 2006 veteran U.S. Pollster Bob Shrum gave a speech attacking Cameron and advocating a strategy to beat him electorally based on his experience of dealing with George Bush and the Republican party. The private event's Smith Institute invited audience included Brownite allies from the Labour party and the media. The outcry at the revelation led to a Charity Commission investigation into partisan activity.

Guardian columnist Polly Toynbee is on the board of the Smith Institute. In March 2005 prior to the 2005 general election she advised a team of Brownite Labour MPs at a Smith Institute event on Tory tactics. Also attending were – surprise, surprise – Deborah Mattinson and Scarlett McGwire from Opinion Leader Research. Ed Balls said at the event he was "very taken by Polly's language in terms of a need for a legend for the left."

Ed Balls left his post as Gordon Brown's special-adviser to campaign in the general election to become an MP. He was given a sinecure at the Smith Institute and paid a sum approaching £100,000 to produce a couple of pamphlets. During this period Konrad Caulkett, a paid employee of the Smith Institute, helped him campaign in his constituency. Konrad was recruited to the Smith Institute by Sarah Macaulay, also known as Mrs Brown.

In December 2004, John Healey MP, Economic Secretary, HM Treasury, told attendees at a Smith Institute seminar "I am a last-minute substitute for Gordon Brown, so I would like, on his behalf, to welcome you all to Number 11 Downing Street. I know, looking around, some of you are quite regular attenders of Smith Institute seminars, and you will know you get a letter from Wilf Stevenson before each one explaining that you are invited to Number 11 by kind permission of the Chancellor. I have to say, this series of seminars in particular is being held not so much by the kind permission of the Chancellor, but by his absolute insistence that they take place. He is unable to be with us now, but he will want to know exactly what has been said in the discussion when I see him later this morning. Many of you, including and perhaps especially the panel here, have known Gordon for a long time."

Guido Fawkes www.order-order.com

New Labour Sleaze in . . .

2007

Gordon and Tony's Sleazeometer, 2007

14 sleazy episodes already and its only June

Not Working – Family Tax Credits
Damon Lambert

Many of you would have thought that parliament was the place where ministers could be held to account for policy implementation and running of their department. Not our Gordon Brown though. A man given to shoving his oar into other people's department is not fond of talking about his own. Despite making great play of introducing the Tax Credit system Gordon has a great aversion to popping along to the Commons and answering at least one question on the topic. You would have thought the PM-elect would have been his usual, "I've seen off 5 Shadow Chancellors" self hard man, desperate to jump in the ring and land a few on Dave (well, us grammar school boys would certainly fall prey to the latter temptation). But the Clunking Fist became a Flunking Mist as Brown bottles the fight every time. Whilst the side-effect of making John Reid jealous amuses, Brown had to take the desperate measure of having to hide behind Ms Dawn Primarolo's skirt in parliament, as she took the flak and Opposition queries whilst he sat next to her Chinese Whispering their excuses.

But Dawn has form too. In Primarololand, the tax credit system works well, has always worked well, and has always been at war with Eurasia. Repeatedly since 2003, and very publicly in 2005, the OverPaymaster General has stated that the Tax Credit system was "stable and performing well" but in May 2007 the all-party Public Affairs Committee concluded that "Tax credits suffer from the highest rates of error and fraud in government" and "The Department does not have up to date information on levels of claimant error and fraud in tax credits".

Her claims just did not tie in with the facts that must have been at her disposal. She even admitted in 2005 that she had known the extent of the problems. In 2004 she said that tax credit overpayments written off were in the region of £37m. It turned out, for that year, to be £1.9bn. In 2005 the Parliamentary Ombudsman held her up for not providing full responses. She claimed that 3% of phone calls to the helplines were unanswered when alternative evidence showed that 22% were. There were 15 unanswered Parliamentary Questions on the topic from one MP alone. The Department refuses to issue up to date information on the costs of errors and rectifying them. Given the loyalty between Chancellor and Minister, Brown knew all this as well as Primarolo. There's something amiss, and not just some hard-up family's cash, when Tony Blair is so moved that he apologises for Gordon's cock-up.

Rather than be man enough to admit there were huge problems and take the drastic measures to rectify them, Team Brown prefers for the lowest paid to bear the impact of an error strewn system and for fraud to continue. Incompetence is one thing, but letting the poorest suffer rather than admit that your own Ministry is failing is a triumph of personal egos over the greater good; an act of selfishness that ranks among New Labour's very sleaziest moments.

Taxcutter http://thetaxcutter.blogspot.com

The Smith Institute:
Gordon Brown's Personal Charity
Guido Fawkes

Back in February 2007 there was pressure building for an explanation as to the Smith Institute's use of No. 11 Downing Street. The fact that the charity seemed to have only one beneficiary – Gordon Brown – meant that it was not only breaking the rules against political activity by a charity, it was actually functioning as a factional powerbase for Brownites. The staff and trustees were all allies of the Chancellor and it forever seemed to hold events to showcase Gordon in the best possible light.

Gordon Brown's political opponents in parliament had tabled parliamentary question after parliamentary question, all were met with stonewalling by the Treasury. Freedom of Information requests were ignored and went unanswered. Then came a breakthrough, the revelation that at a private meeting of the Smith Institute, attended by a long list of Brownite allies in the media and the Labour party, the U.S. pollster Bob Shrum had advised on a strategy to defeat David Cameron's Conservatives based on his experience fighting the Republican party. The speech transcript was proof that the allegations were well founded.

I made a formal complaint under Section 8 of the Charities Act. The Charity Commission indicated that it would consider taking action. It leaked out before the official announcement was made that they would commence a formal inquiry. This led to a flurry of activity at the Smith Institute and HM Treasury. Their response was transparently choreographed in the knowledge that a statutory inquiry under the Charities Act would bring previously suppressed documents and information into the public domain.

After months of pressure it was suddenly revealed that nearly two hundred meetings had been held by the Smith Institute (free of charge) at No. 11 Downing Street with the permission of the Chancellor. I had been alleging that the use of the building effectively amounted to a subsidy of the Smith Institutes' activities by HM Treasury. It was literally an abuse of office in all senses of the word.

In those circumstances if it were to have been revealed that the Treasury had made direct payments to the Smith Institute, Gordon Brown's political front group, it would have been extremely damaging. The charge against Brown that he was corruptly financing his political ambitions would be hard to defend.

Amazingly a letter dated February 1, 2007, and written by Paul Myners was produced to explain away just such a payment. Myners is a Smith Institute trustee, a Treasury appointed veteran of various Gordon Brown created quangos, who is considered a safe pair of hands by Brownites. He was also a wealthy donor to Gordon's leadership campaign.

It explained that over two years previously the Treasury had paid the Smith Institute £11,750 to hold two seminars on behalf of the Myners Review into the financial sector for Gordon. It went on to claim (without explanation) that the Treasury had paid the money by mistake. That it was always Myners' intention to pay the cost himself. That he had now, over two years later, paid the sum personally.

If the Charity Commission investigation was not going to bring knowledge of this payment into the public domain, there is no doubt that the Treasury payment to the Smith Institute would have been kept well hidden with no danger of it being discovered or repaid.

The explanations given by Myners are frankly incredible. He expects us to believe that the Smith Institute *accidentally* invoiced HM Treasury and that HM Treasury accidentally paid the invoice. We are asked to believe that suddenly two years later he decided to pay the bill having told his "team that I would be happy to personally contribute some or all of the costs of the seminars". But he didn't actually do it at the time, did he?

Why the Two Year Interval? Could it be that the imminent and inevitable exposure of the payment by HM Treasury to the Smith Institute during the course of the Charity Commission's investigation was the real and only reason the payment was now refunded by Myners to the Treasury? It was a plain and simple cover up – long after the event – by Myners to help his friend Gordon Brown out of a politically difficult situation.

Guido Fawkes, www.order-order.com

A New Kind of Politics, ahem
(Gordon's SpAds)
Ed Thomas

Gordon Brown recently told the *Guardian* of his plans for "a new kind of politics in this country ... a new style of government in the future. If you believed in the past that you could have a top-down approach and a government that simply pulled the levers, that is not how it is going to work in the future."

Ah yes, that's the spirit. Gone all those little cabals of spinmeisters and think-tanks. Gone the Anthony Giddens worship. So long, and thanks for all the finagling.

Ah, but. Not quite. Honestly, not at all.

For there Gordon was just pulling the old spin trick. The very essence of the top-down approach is the attempt to work the media to deceive the public, and that's just what he was doing.

I mean, isn't he blatant? He's already elevated two of his Special Advisors – Ed Milliband and Ed Balls – to the fast-track of Labour politics, slipping them into safe seats and grooming them for his top jobs. A new style of politics, rather like the old one with knobs on.

According to the *Guardian*, most reliable mouthpiece of the spin monster when the message is really sickly, "Mr Brown wants a cull of "spin doctors" – particularly special advisers."

The catch is that he would like to see "other special adviser jobs going to people who have detailed expertise in policy".

Ah yes, detailed experience in policy given to them by... da, da, da, Gordon Brown, who created such edifices as the Smith Institute, an economic think tank registered as a charitable organisation, which meets frequently at Number Eleven Downing Street so as to keep people of Balls' ilk close to big Gs' heart.

There was also the Council of Economic Advisors, set up by Brown as an adjunct to his special advisors, to keep another set of groupies nice and close at hand.

Just ask former key Brown spinner Charlie Whelan. Charlie says, "Brown keeps his cards closer to his chest than Blair does and his coterie is tighter."

Is this beginning to sound like a recipe for fresh and open government? Thought not.

In fact, the CoEA seems to have a highly presidential flavour, since the same title was accorded to a group of great importance created by US Federal law in 1946 precisely to promote "top-down" economic manage-ment. Gordon, it seems, likes to go large with his deceits.

Among others, expect to see Shriti Vadera, head of the CoEA, and Wilf Stevenson, head of the Smith Institute, among Gordon's bosom pals. These people have been around since the beginning of Gordon's days in office, and they are about to get a great big leg up in their careers.

It does seem a far cry from the days when every media outlet to the left of the *Telegraph* – and even some of them at the *Telegraph* – was criticising Mrs Thatcher for relying on advisors such as Professor Sir Alan Walters. It was innovatory, then. These days "SpAds" are an industry of their own, and a distinctly cabbalistic, unfree enterprise.

But I will leave it to Hansard (24 May 2007!) to demonstrate as only history can how much Gordon Brown represents "fresh government". You shall see how Gordon has stuck firmly to the principle of Government by an elite, for, well, you have a think about it. Take it away, Baroness Noakes:

"Mr Ed Balls. Having worked for Gordon Brown in opposition, in 1997 he was appointed as the Chancellor's economic adviser, which was a special adviser post. Two years later, he crossed over into the Civil Service and became the Chancellor's chief economic adviser; he stayed there until 1995, when he became a parliamentary candidate for the seat that he now holds. Did anybody believe that Mr Balls was anything other than a political adviser to the Chancellor throughout that whole period? I think not.

In addition, the Chancellor has a Council of Economic Advisers, which has been estimated to cost more than £1 million a year. Five of its members are appointed on special adviser terms. Why did the Chancellor find it necessary to gather advisers around him in this way when he was surrounded by the undoubted intellects who exist in large numbers among Treasury civil servants? Has the advice of his civil servants been replaced and, if so, why was that necessary?"

Yup. A real fresh broom is sweeping in, restoring trust to Parliament and the Civil Service. I suddenly feel decidedly queasy.

Biased BBC http://biased-bbc.blogspot.com

A Junketing They Will Go
Chris Doidge

In the foreword to the must-read 'Teach Yourself Caravanning', Margaret Beckett reveals how she loves to go for a trip to the Continent with her husband Leo. Not only is it "luxurious", it is also environmentally friendly.

They would stay in the caravan while at the party conference in Blackpool, and travel the length and breadth of Britain and France. Sadly 'security reasons' have made this less practical while Mrs Beckett is in her current job.

But it's a pity for the environment, caravan sites the world over, and of course the taxpayer, that Mrs Beckett and husband seem to have instead developed a love of holidays paid for by the British taxpayer.

While her predecessors Jack Straw and Robin Cook occasionally took their wives abroad with them, Mrs Beckett seems to have become rather homesick while Foreign Secretary, taking Leo away with her on eight foreign trips in her first six months in the job.

These holidays are, of course, for official government business. But you might question the use of 79-year old Leo Beckett when his wife is discussing climate change or the Middle East and schmoozing with world leaders.

Mrs Beckett tops the list when it comes to spending her Parliamentary allowance on staff, at £100,000. Naturally, the fact that Leo is one of her Parliamentary staff can mean it is only coincidental that she needs plenty of help around the office.

The ministerial code says that spouses should only go on junkets with their partners 'occasionally', but Mr Beckett's role as a paid adviser seems to mean he can get around the rules.

But what is his role? Officially he's in charge of Mrs Beckett's constituency office. But unofficially, he's a permanent fixture at the Foreign Office, rarely leaving civil servants alone with his wife.

Would it be unfair to suggest that work experience is a little unnecessary at Mr Beckett's age. Or to point out that it usually doesn't offer such a hefty salary?

www.chrisdoidge.co.uk

The Birmingham Terror Raids
Mike Anson

January 31 2007 saw the newspaper headlines looking bad for New Labour and Number 10. Lord Levy had just been re-arrested in the cash-for-honours scandal. He had been questioned for more than four hours on suspicion of conspiracy to pervert the course of justice. In the previous week Mr. Blair had also been questioned by police for a second time on the same issue. Knowledge of Mr. Blair's interview was not public at that point, having been kept quiet for "operational reasons".

Fortunately for Mr. Blair and New Labour, the next day's headlines were dominated by a different story. At 4am that morning, police arrested nine men in the Birmingham area. There was an alleged plot to kidnap and behead a Muslim member of the British Army live on the internet. The newspapers led with prurient detail of the alleged plot and the arrests. Certain newspapers appeared to be very well informed.

Perhaps it was merely an amazing coincidence, but news of Mr. Blair's second questioning by police was released that same day. Strangely, it was pushed from the front pages by the media frenzy surrounding the terrorist arrests.

Little more was made of this sequence of events until a lecture was given in April 2007 by Deputy Assistant

Commissioner Peter Clarke, head of the Anti-Terrorism Branch of the Metropolitan Police. DAC Clarke made a number of surprising and pointed statements:

"What I am talking about is the deliberate leaking of highly sensitive operational intelligence, often classified, and the unauthorised release of which can be a criminal offence. I make no allegations about the source of leaks or about individual cases. What is clear is that there are a number, a small number I am sure, of misguided individuals who betray confidences.

Perhaps they look to curry favour with certain journalists, or to squeeze out some short term presentational advantage – I do not know what motivates them. The people who do this either do not know or do not care what damage they do. If they do know, then they are beneath contempt. If they do not know, then let me tell them. They compromise investigations. They reveal sources of life saving intelligence. In the worst cases they put lives at risk. I wonder if they simply do not care.

The recent investigation in Birmingham into an allegation that a British serviceman had been targeted by a terrorist network is but one example of this. On the morning of the arrests, almost before the detainees had arrived at the police stations to which they were being taken for questioning, it was clear that key details of the investigation and the evidence had been leaked. This damaged the interview strategy of the investigators, and undoubtedly raised community tensions. I have no idea where the leaks came from, but whoever was responsible should be thoroughly ashamed of themselves."

Subsequent calls for an inquiry were rejected by Mr. Blair even though it was reported that journalists from one tabloid were briefed about the alleged plot on the night before the arrests. This resulted in some journalists travelling to the scene of the arrests before anyone had actually been arrested. It was further reported that, on that morning whilst one of the suspects remained at large, a small and select number of journalists were receiving detailed briefings on the alleged plot. It also emerged that a "senior government official" told reporters on at least two tabloid newspapers that a number of Muslim soldiers had agreed to act as bait to trap the plotters.

So there you have it. News of Mr. Blair's second questioning by the Police was "buried" on the day that Police arrested nine men in connection with an alleged terrorist plot. To facilitate the old New Labour trick of "burying bad news", selected newspapers were briefed with prurient and perhaps classified details. This ensured no unwelcome headlines or press coverage of Mr. Blair would be heard through the noise. In fact those newspapers were so well informed, or alternatively blessed with clairvoyance, that journalists were dispatched to Birmingham to report on the terror-raids before the police had in fact arrested anyone or the raids had taken place.

In the usual New Labour trick of obfuscation and attacking an unwelcome question, but at the same time totally missing its point; when asked at Prime Minister's

Questions whether the government would establish an independent leak inquiry, Mr. Blair responded "No, I will not confirm that, for this very simple reason. If you have evidence that someone has been involved in such a thing I will of course have it properly investigated".

Isn't finding this evidence the point of such an inquiry? Unless of course, that inquiry would lead back to No.10, or perhaps, more likely, the Home Office.

Anyone but Gordon http://anyonebutgordon.blogspot.com

Britain's Favourite Lawyer
Martin Curtis

Lord Goldsmith was appointed to the post of Attorney General in 2001, amid some controversy; mainly because many felt that his inexperience in International Law meant that he was not suitable for the post, whilst his links with the Labour Party made him look suspiciously like another one of Tony's cronies.

In the run up to the Iraq War the opinion of the Attorney General was pivotal. His final view was that an invasion without a UN mandate was legal. There was a mass of voices asking for his legal advice to be published, and with some justification because it was suspected that he had a rapid turnaround in his own thinking. Before the war it is alleged that he had advised some of his friends in the legal profession that he had doubts about the legality of invading Iraq, yet at the crucial point he came out in support of the man who appointed him. When his early advice was inevitably leaked it did indeed show a number of reservations about the legal case for war. This early advice was written on 7th March, his final advice supporting the case was made on 17th March, a turnaround within a period of just ten days. In his only appearance at the Cabinet in the run up to the War, Ministers were allegedly not given the opportunity to question him. Lord Goldsmith would of course deny that he succumbed to pressure.

Lord Goldsmith was also the man who sanctioned the decision to halt investigations into corruption by BAe Systems, who were alleged to have placed bribes in the run up to being awarded the contract for the Al Yamamah project by the Saudi Government. It is apparently not in the National interest to investigate cases of corruption.

It seems almost inevitable that someone surrounded by so much sleaze would have had an affair; earlier this year Lord Goldsmith admitted an extra-marital liaison with Britain's first female Indian Q.C.

Lord Goldsmith's may find himself with another place in the sleaze hall of fame through his involvement in the Cash for Honours scandal where, despite his closeness to those at the centre of the investigations, he has remorselessly asserted his right to make the final decision on prosecutions. The Director of the Crown Prosecution Service has done the honourable thing and confirmed that he would not be involved in any decision because of a conflict of interest, but Lord Goldsmith remains determined to have his say. Given that he has already sanctioned the abandonment of one corruption enquiry, there is legitimate cause for concern.

Spin Blog, www.spinblog.co.uk

Cherie Blair and the £25,000 Speech

Ellee Seymour

Cherie Blair amassed a fortune as a lucrative lecture-tour celebrity speaker, cashing in on her privileged position as the wife of the British Prime Minister.

But surely she could have foretold the furore that her £25,000 fee for spending five hours at an event sponsored by the family of Osama Bin Laden would have caused.

It led to accusations that she was breaking Whitehall's anti-sleaze rules as under Whitehall's Ministerial code, the political status of Ministers must not be used to allow their spouses to earn money.

Yet her appearance was actively promoted by the organisers as the wife of the British Prime Minister, and not solely in her professional name, Cherie Booth QC.

She was accompanied on the trip to Jeddah, the Saudi Arabian home of the Al Qaeda leader's immensely rich family, by two Scotland Yard bodyguards and a Downing Street adviser – all paid for by the British taxpayer, along with the diplomat who collected her from the airport.

These disclosures in March, 2007 were particularly embarrassing to No 10 as they came in the wake of Blair's halting of a Serious Fraud Office probe into corruption claims concerning a Saudi arms deal with Britain's BAe Systems.

One of the main backers of the Jeddah Economic Forum, which invited Cherie Blair as a human rights attorney and because of her high profile position, was the Bin Laden group, set up by Osama Bin Laden's father and now the largest construction firm in the Islamic world.

Although the family disowned Osama in 1994, some members are rumoured to have retained contact with him.

The visit led to Tory spokesman Chris Grayling questioning Cherie's lack of judgement, and he said:

"Under the Ministerial rules, the Prime Minister has to separate his family's financial interests from his job. Once again, it looks as though this has not happened, which is certainly a breach of the spirit of the Ministerial code and probably is a breach of the code itself.

"The suggestion that she went to Saudi Arabia just as a human rights lawyer simply doesn't ring true. Mr Blair should declare this money in the Commons Register of Interests immediately and apologise for not doing so at the time."

Ellee Seymour www.elleeseymour.com

Not so sleazy does it...

Chris Mounsey

I n Scotland, May's local elections were something of a mixed bag with the SNP winning only a single seat more than Labour in the Parliament. However, the local election results were mired in scandal.

A new system – the single transferable vote – was employed to elect the councillors and, rather more importantly, a new system of electronic counting (e-counting) of the ballots was used.

And it was a fiasco. To say that the machines were not quite up to the task seems something of an understatement – comparisons were drawn with the infamous "hanging chads" debacle in the US presidential elections. Counts were severely delayed as the machines struggled to cope and thousands of papers were discarded as spoiled.

Indeed, in a number of areas – such as in Airdrie and Shotts, where the 1,536 spoiled ballots was more than the 1,446 Labour majority – the combination of the new voting system and the new counting machines led to some potentially serious anomalies. The Electoral Reform Society condemned the situation as "shocking and intolerable."

As ever, there is another angle. The poorly functioning e-counting machines were provided by DRS Data Services; the company was selected by the ruling Labour administration and we are sure that it is mere coincidence that one of the DRS Directors is former Vice-President of the EU Commission and erstwhile Labour leader, Neil Kinnock.

But does this really count as sleaze? One could argue that it is not (unless of course, you think that a political party assigning a contract to a company in which a former leader of that same party is involved). Instead, let us give them the benefit of the doubt and assume that there was actually a tender and that DRS Data Services won fair and square.

But the fact remains that the e-counting did not work as planned – counts were delayed and the results left in doubt – and so the taxpayers' money paid to DRS was, effectively, wasted. As usual with almost anything that Kinnock has ever been involved with, this is less an example of sleaze and more a typical example of utter incompetence.

But then, these days we really shouldn't be surprised at New Labour's propensity for chucking our money away on grandiose and superfluous IT projects.

Devil's Kitchen http://devilskitchen.me.uk

Communication doesn't come cheap...
Chris Mounsey

With a salary not far shy of £60,000, average expenses of some £130,000, an office running costs allowance of £20,000 and a prepaid envelope allowance of £7,000, one might be forgiven for thinking that MPs had all that they needed to communicate effectively with their constituents.

In March 2007, our elected representatives in the House of Commons voted to allocate themselves a £10,000 Communications Allowance to spend on websites and the like. Although some Tory and LibDem MPs voted for it too, it received the support of a huge majority of Labour MPs, particularly those in marginal seats.

This is, essentially, a propaganda budget.

Let us leave aside the fact that apparently many MPs are so utterly ineffective that they need to convince their constituents that they are actually doing something to earn their massive salaries and attendant perks, and focus instead on what this budget is actually for.

It is a budget for MPs to tell their voters what a very fine job they are doing. It is, in other words, a £10,000 per year electoral advantage that the incumbent MP has over any challenger, thus entrenching their own position.

In other words, even though their material will not be allowed to contain party information, it does effectively help the incumbent party MP maintain the status quo, both for themselves and their party.

Labour's Jack Straw MP maintained that this was not the case. "The purpose of this allowance is to contribute to better public understanding of what this Parliament is about and what it does... It's important for the health of our democracy for the public to know more about what we do."

Straw added it was "not to become a propaganda tool for the use of incumbents" and it was time to "make clear what the rules are".

The only rule that MPs seem to understand is that they have control over vast amounts of our money and that all they have to do to gain access to it is to vote themselves a new perk or allowance. And these allowances are not even as fixed as one might hope: in 2005/06, the average claim on postage was £4,000 but Labour's Andrew Dismore claimed over £25,000.

And no matter what Jack Straw may tell us, this allowance will be used for shameless self-promotion. We are used to politicians grandstanding: and now they have more of our money to help them do so.

Devil's Kitchen http://devilskitchen.me.uk

It may not be a fish but it still smells
Phil Hendren

As the Labour leadership battle began to hot up in the wake of Blair's confirmation that he wouldn't be leader at the 2007 Labour Conference, there were so many names floated as big hitting challengers to Gordon Brown it began to look increasingly likely he would face a contest for the crown to which he'd been waiting for so long. At the same time as the media speculation ran rampant, the small media company that produced the "Dave the Chameleon" adverts for the Labour Party's 2006 local election campaign, Silverfish TV, was busy purchasing an array of Internet domain names which were identifiable to the Chosen One Brown.

On October 26th 2006, the assistant producer at Silverfish, Rachel Bull purchased, amongst others, gordonbrownforleader.com, .org, .co.uk, as well as gordonbrownforbritain.com, etc etc. To list them all here would be a waste of reading time, but you get the picture. These Internet addresses laid empty, waiting and unknown until April 11th 2007 when some were exposed on this writer's blog. On that day, Silverfish TV's corporate website openly boasted about its heavily political client list. They proudly talked up the work they had done for not just the Labour Party and a number of Trade Unions, but also Her Majesty's Treasury. However, this would change very soon as the story developed.

As the news spread that Gordon Brown appeared to be preparing for a leadership contest, Cathy Newman at Channel 4 News followed the story up. She was told by Silverfish TV that the domain names were bought speculatively as there was a "mini-industry" in such things. The implication being that they would sell them to Brown when the time came for a healthy profit (something which is against the rules governing the Internet but this is by the by). Meanwhile, the Treasury vehemently denied having anything to Silverfish TV, ever.

At the same time, the *Times* newspaper began to ask questions around the story. Its diary columnist, Hugo Rifkind, spoke to the Treasury about the contradiction between what Silverfish were saying on their website and the Treasury's denial that they had nothing to do with the company. Whilst the Treasury continued with its vehement denials, they also said that the contradictions were "less straightforward than it seems". Meanwhile the Silverfish TV website had been taken offline and simply displayed a announcement that it was "Under Construction". Within days the website re-appeared with a revised client list sans the Treasury. The phrase "he who controls history controls the future" springs readily to mind doesn't it?

However, it was almost a month later before Gordon Brown's leadership campaign was finally launched with the name "Gordon Brown For Britain". And where was the location of the accompanying campaign website you may ask? That's right, it was on one of the many domains registered by Silverfish TV's Rachel Bull the previous October, where it remains at the time of writing. The domain remains under the ownership of the Labour-friendly company that registered it speculatively to sell to Brown, a company which Brown and the Treasury have honestly never had anything to do with!

Move along, nothing to see here.

Dizzy Thinks http://dizzythinks.net

Balls to Tony: It's Gordon's crony!
Chris Mounsey

Colin Challen was elected to the Commons in the 2001 General Election, representing the constituency of Morley and Rothwell. In 2006, boundary changes ensured that his seat was to be merged with another and became Morley and Outwood.

At this time, two people put their names forward to represent New Labour in this seat: Challen and Gordon Brown favourite, Ed Balls. Boundary changes were also due to rearrange Balls' seat of Normanton, with a third of it being merged into Morley and Outwood.

Ed Balls is the Economic Secretary to the Treasury and a close confidante of Prime-Minister-in-waiting, Gordon Brown; indeed, Balls has served as an economic advisor to Brown, in one capacity or another, since 1994.

In November 2006, Challen announced that he would fight Balls for the seat. "I shall be seeking to be re-elected as the Labour candidate – if I were successful I would be representing a seat that contains two thirds of my existing seat."

And yet, only two months later, Challen announced that he would not be contesting the next general election – focusing his efforts on climate change instead – and leaving the way clear for Ed Balls to contest the seat for Labour.

What could possibly have made Challen change his mind?

The answer came in February 2007, when Sir Nicholas Stern – author of the deeply suspect Stern Review on climate change and now heading up a climate change panel – revealed that it was Gordon Brown who had appointed Challen to the taskforce; Stern also admitted that he had had no prior knowledge of the appointment.

It was impossible to shake the suspicion that Gordon Brown, unable to face losing his Balls, had effectively given Challen with a sinecure in order to persuade him to stand aside.

In an addendum to the story, Danny Finkelstein of *The Times* took blogger Iain Dale to task for suggesting that this was anything other than realpolitik. "Iain suggests that Gordon Brown's behaviour and my cynical acceptance of it is the sort of thing that puts people off politics. Let me put an alternative point – blowing up trivial and perfectly sensible political moves into pseudo-scandals and going on about them is what puts people off politics."

Actually the real scandal here is that yet another person with absolutely no scientific qualifications, nor any specialist economic knowledge, should be appointed to a powerful advisory panel on climate change simply to clear the way for the Chancellor's boot-boy.

Devil's Kitchen http://devilskitchen.me.uk

Shoot that Golden Arrow through my heart!
Phil Hendren

In March 2007, New Labour found itself, yet again, embroiled in a "cash for access" scandal. An undercover reporter had landed a job at the lobbyist, Golden Arrow Communications, and allegations had surfaced against two ministers, Gerry Sutcliffe (Prisons) and Stephen Ladyman (Transport). It was alleged that Sutcliffe had offered his Whitehall diary to the lobbyists, whilst Ladyman was said to have leaked highly confidential information about road charging plans.

The Golden Arrow consultant Ivan Henderson was taped saying of Ladyman that, "[e]very time I e-mail him, he comes right back... He says 'Ivan, this is what the score is'. He has never turned me down yet. He has gone over the top really. It is a bit dodgy sometimes." He went on to tell the undercover reporter that Sutcliffe had offered himself to Golden Arrow telling them "Come on, you use me....I am there to be used. I want to help you. Use me."

A curious reader might wonder why two ministers would offer themselves so freely to a public affairs company? After all, when even the lobbyists call it "dodgy" you have to wonder don't you? Could it be because the person saying it, Ivan Henderson, is the former Labour MP for Harwich and currently the prospective parliamentary candidate for the new seat of

Clacton? Or perhaps it was because his colleague at Golden Arrow at the time was David Jamieson?

If you're wondering who that is, that would be the same David Jamieson, who was the MP for Plymouth Devonport until 2005. He was also a minister at the Department of Transport, but I'm sure that it's just a coincidence he's working for a transport lobbying company. Nothing "dodgy" here please move along. Jamieson's most famous time of course came when, as the Minister for Road Safety, he was interviewed whilst someone was being run over by a lorry just over his shoulder.

Now I should say there are actually rules in place that require ex-Ministers to clear their new jobs with the Civil Service first. Unfortunately, David Jamieson 'forgot'. Easy enough to do I guess, all that wining and dining whilst reportedly charging to £250 an hour to... errr... phone his ex-colleagues at the Department for Transport must be quite taxing on the memory I imagine.

Whilst we're on the rules, there's also a professional code of conduct that lobbying firms sign up to. This includes rules dictating, for example, that lobbyists should not hold Parliamentary passes. However, seeing as Ivan Henderson was registered as a sponsored pass holder on behalf of Golden Arrow by the Labour MP, Tony Wright, it's likely they don't think the code of conduct is for them.

Tony who? you may be asking. He's the Labour MP for Great Yarmouth. Before Ivan Henderson was his "researcher/lobbyist" he had a different researcher called

Ian Woodcroft. Sadly Ian decided to leave and become a Senior Account Executive responsible for political research at errr.. Golden Arrow Communications. Incidentally, did I mention that the MD of Golden Arrow is Andrew Sharp, formerly a regional organiser for the Labour Party who also worked at Labour HQ on the Nolan Bill that governed political financial contributions? No? Oh well, you know now.

Dizzy Thinks http://dizzythinks.net

Liam Byrne: Caring and Sharing
Chris Mounsey

L iam Byrne was a former aide to Tony Blair – although probably one of thousands! – who found himself in hot water over the 21,000 shares that he owned in E-Government Solutions Ltd (EGS).

EGS – which was founded by Byrne and describes itself as "the UK's leading provider of e-commerce exchanges for trading with the public sector" – has contracts with eight police forces and is bidding for more. In the last year, EGS turned over £1.4 million.

So far, so good: it is, it could be argued, beneficial that at least a few members of our ruling class have some experience of business; further, the remittance that Mr Byrne was paid as a member of the supervisory board of the EGS Group was hardly a fortune, being between £10k and £15k.

But there was a small problem.

At the time of going to print, Liam Byrne is a Minister for Immigration at the Home Office, which is responsible for the police. A fairly tenuous connection – the Home Office is a large department – and it is unlikely that Mr Byrne would have made an appearance in this book had he not actually been Police Minister at the time that EGS were picking up contracts.

The expenses-campaigning Liberal Democrat MP, Norman Baker, pointed out that, "Mr Byrne is very well connected to the Blair project and therefore would doubtless have come across issues relating to conflicts of interest as they have permeated the Blair Government. Mr Byrne would have been much wiser to have disposed of his shares immediately upon taking ministerial office..."

However, in a statement published by a Home Office aide on 3 June 2007, an aide stated that, "Mr Byrne has played no role in the procurement process whatsoever, so he has had no idea about any of the negotiations that might be taking place. There is no conflict of interest."

It remains to be seen whether anyone believes him. Don't hold your breath...

Devil's Kitchen http://devilskitchen.me.uk

Gordon Brown: Master of Spin
Iain Dale

T wo hundred and forty three years after the invention of the SPINNING JENNY we seem to have discovered its modern day equivalent, the Spinning Gordon.

In *TIME* Magazine in early June 2007 award winning photographer Tom Stoddart did a gushing photo essay that subsequently appeared in various papers including both *The Sun* and *The Mirror*. The spin Brown's people put on this was that Gordon travelled on a rush hour train with ordinary people. His team then made sure that the girl to his left on the train offered quotes to the few journalists in attendance. Clearly Brown's people were pushing this as him being an 'ordinary Londoner'. Sadly it was complete rubbish.

1. It wasn't rush hour it was late morning on the way to his launch event
2. He surrounded himself with friendly Labour activists and then sat there ignoring them in an attempt to look normal
3. He spent the previous week talking about how he wanted to see an end to spin

Something troubled me about the photo when I saw it. Sue Nye (Mrs Gavin Davies), his Political Secretary, was sitting to his right on the train, but the girl on his left was not exactly an ordinary member of the public either. She was Rohini Simbodyal, a 20 year old student at the London School of Oriental and African Studies. But not only that.

Rohini was backing Hazel Blears for the Deputy Leadership and is the Youth and Student Officer for the Enfield Young Labour Party. She is also chair of the SOAS Labour Party and is the black, minority and ethnic officer for Labour students. Clearly not just an average punter on the tube!

This is how she was quoted in the media...

"Brown took the London subway, known as the Tube, to the event, impressing at least one student, Rohini Simbodyal."We got on the Tube and people were looking at Gordon Brown," Simbodyal, 20, said. "People were amazed, saying: 'It's Gordon.' But everyone was very British, they looked and then looked away. A few people came up and shook his hand and said 'Good luck.' "He was just like a normal guy," she said.

She also appeared in one of Brown's video pieces on his campaign site.

OK, so it's not exactly Watergate, but if the era of spin is over, why was Gordon Brown's campaign resorting to these sort of tactics to make him look like a common punter? It's not clever and it backfires.

A few days later various stories appeared in the Sunday newspapers about how Gordon was going to get tough on terror. What the journalists writing those stories didn't tell you was how this story got into their papers.

Gordon Brown's spinner-in-chief Damian McBride and Michael Ellams spent most of Saturday phoning round the Sunday lobby giving them 'exclusive' insights into Gordon Brown's views on fighting terrorism. I believe there was even a document from which the journalists were able to craft their words. Indeed, so similar were the stories in the main broadsheets they *had* to have been given a document. Now, nothing wrong with that until you know what the terms of this 'exclusive' story were.

Brown's spinners told at least one of these papers that they would only get the story if they agreed not to carry any quotes from David Davis, Nick Clegg or any other opposition spokesman. Not only that, they weren't even allowed to tell the Tories or LibDems about the very existence of the story. Consequently not a single one of the stories in any of the broadsheets contained a quote from David Davis or Nick Clegg. Coincidence? No.

At 7.30pm on Saturday night the Press Association got hold of the story from one of the nationals. They hadn't been included in the 'briefings' from McBride. They wrote the story complete with an extensive quote from David Davis, yet not a single Sunday paper carried it. Davis pointed out that Brown's intervention threatened to blow apart the cross-party discussions which had been going on between Blair and Cameron, and himself, Reid and Clegg. Newsworthy? I think so.

The fact is that Blair and Cameron had reached agreement on a way forward on using phone tap evidence in court, and Davis had negotiated a way forward with Reid in a number of other areas. It was all set to be announced this Thursday by Reid in a Commons Statement.

Brown's intervention cut across all of this. Reid was left fuming spluttering about Brown playing politics with terrorism and using it for his own purposes. He could hardly be blamed. He was completely undermined by Brown's activities.

You won't, of course, read this version of events in any of the mainstream newspapers, because if you did, they'd be struck off Gordon's briefing list. Make no mistake, the media are waking up to the fact that Gordon's spinning regime will be just as ruthless as it was under Alastair Campbell and Peter Mandelson. They are spinning exactly the opposite, of course, which just makes it even worse. One day, perhaps, the lobby will stop co-operating with their bullying tactics.

Iain Dale's Diary http://iaindale.blogpsot.com

And Also . . .

Coining It
Peter Cuthbertson

Disgraced ministers have returned to office following scandals before New Labour came to power. But it took Tony Blair to truly pioneer the technique of bringing back ministers who resigned over sleaze only to lose the *same* minister to sleaze once again. This cavalier attitude to using character references when re-hiring has not only guaranteed further scandals and abuse of office by unreformed ministers such as David Blunkett and Peter Mandelson, but has ensured the scandal of these ministers earning enough severance pay in a short space of time to qualify as a second income.

Owing to a system that began in 1991, Cabinet Ministers are entitled to a quarter of their annual incomes as severance pay when they resign. It is unlikely that this means of guarding against retiring Cabinet Ministers facing precipitous falls in income after leaving office was designed with the aim of boosting the bank balances of those who resigned multiple times in disgrace. But by doing so, David Blunkett and Peter Mandelson were able to milk the system for all it was worth.

For resigning from four different cabinet posts during New Labour's first two terms, Blunkett and Mandelson were able to split between them more than £60,000 of taxpayers' money in severance payments. Mandelson's first resignation over the home loans scandal brought a payoff off at least

£11,000 – and Stephen Byers, his successor as Trade and Industry Secretary, confirmed the final figure could be as much as £15,412. His swift return to office, and then the accompanying resignation over the Hinduja passports scandal, netted Mandelson a further £12,129.

David Blunkett did even better for himself, taking £18,725 for his December 2004 resignation for speeding up the visa application for his lover's foreign nanny, and netting another £18,725 just 11 months later when forced to resign from his new position after his links to the firm DNA Bioscience.

Even in the (brief) intervening period before Blair brought him back as Work and Pensions Secretary, Blunkett was to live at the taxpayers' considerable expense in the £3 million Belgravia mansion intended for the use of *sitting* Cabinet Ministers. The annual rent for such a home, owned legitimately by any private citizen, would be about £150,000 – plus an extra £50,000 in taxes. David Blunkett was paying neither.

In case anyone thought this scandalous abuse of taxpayers' funds was over, it has to be recalled that in 2004 Tony Blair returned Peter Mandelson to office an incredible third time, sending him to Brussels to be Britain's EU Commissioner, responsible for Europe's trade policy. Along with all the perks Eurocrats receive at all levels, Peter Mandelson can look forward to his gold-plated EU pension after he leaves office – even if for once, this time, he manages to do so legitimately.

www.concom.blogspot.com

Constituencies for Coronets
Paul Linford

L ong before it was alleged that Tony Blair had handed out seats in the House of Lords in return for loans to the Labour Party or help in establishing his flagship city academies the whiter-than-white one was busy abusing the honours system for political purposes. The business of becoming a Labour peer under Blair has often had less to do with merit and more to do with whether you have a safe Commons seat available for one of his favourites.

It doesn't always work. Before the 1997 election, Blair persuaded the long-serving Dudley MP Sir John Gilbert to step down, on the promise of being made a minister in the Lords, to create a vacancy for his former flatmate and best chum Charlie Falconer.

Unfortunately for him, Falconer bombed at the selection meeting when it emerged that he sent his children to private school, and the PM eventually had to make him a peer too in order to get him into the Government.

Blair was also determined to find a seat for the Tory defector Alan Howarth, who had assumed an importance as a symbol of New Labour's "big tent" style of politics, out of all proportion to his ability.

The veteran Newport East MP Roy Hughes was duly prevailed upon to stand down in his favour, shortly afterwards re-emerging as Lord Islwyn despite having enjoyed a Commons career of stultifying mediocrity.

More recently, in 2001, Blair set about trying to find a way of getting the head of his policy unit, David Miliband, into the Commons, as a necessary precursor to bringing him into the Cabinet.

Eventually the veteran South Shields MP and former Cabinet Minister Dr David Clark agreed to fall on his sword, being rewarded with both a peerage and the chairmanship of the Forestry Commission.

Blair has also attempted to use the honours system as a means of repaying political debts and patching up broken promises.

Back in 1995, he famously persuaded the then Labour Chief Whip, Derek Foster, to stand down, promising him a Cabinet job when Labour returned to Government with the words "and I don't mean a tiddler like Transport". Foster was in fact given a junior ministerial role so menial he resigned it after 48 hours, whereupon he was offered both a peerage and the chairmanship of the soon-to-be-created North-East Development Agency as a consolation prize. To his credit, Foster stood firm before finally taking ermine in 2005.

www.paullinford.blogspot.com

Anyone Got a Match?
Jenny Geddes

In 1997 Labour promised Scotland a "Bonfire of the Quangos". Well, they not only took the piss but poured it over said bonfire. In June 2005 it was revealed the Labour (and LibDem) Executive spent £1.68 billion a year more on quangos than four years previously. Staff numbers had increased by 7,000 in the last year.

And why not? It's a nice earner for Labour hacks.

Take Norman Murray, former Labour convenor of COSLA, for example. He was appointed in 2002 to the Scottish Ambulance Service board at £7,305 a year.

Leading Lanarkshire Labour councillor Harry McGuigan was appointed a member of the Scottish Children's Reporter Administration board.

Former Edinburgh council leader Lesley Hinds and Donald Anderson, the current one, are members of the Health Education Board for Scotland and VisitScotland respectively.

Brian Cavanagh, formerly of Edinburgh council, is the £36,505-a-year chairman of Lothian NHS Board. Mr Cavanagh was discovered allowing Labour politicians to vet Health Board press releases to save political embarrassment.

Formerly of Strathclyde Council, John Mullin was Chairman of NHS Argyll and Clyde. It was so badly run financially that the Executive had to scrap it entirely and split it up between NHS Highland and NHS Greater Glasgow.

Listed as Shettleston Labour members, Professor Alan Alexander and wife Morag did quite well out of our largesse. In 2002 Alan became Chairman of Scottish Water at £70,000 a year for three-and-a-half-days a week. Morag was less lucky only collecting £21,000 a year for her part-time role as convener of the Scottish Social Services Council. Alan has since resigned, having differences of opinion with the Labour-LibDem Executive.

Former Lothian Councillor William Roe couldn't believe his luck when he became Chairman of Highlands & Islands Enterprise since the quango had given his Hebridean software company Mysterian a support package of almost £200,000. Several weeks later it went into administration.

In June 2004 Willie Haughey, who donated hundreds of thousands to Labour, was appointed chairman of Scottish Enterprise Glasgow. In April 2005 Jack McConnell met Haughey to discuss compensation because the M74 would pass through Haughey's property. Initial compensation of £7.4 million rose to £16.5 million. And just this March it was reported that the quango Haughey chairs awarded his company nearly £1 million in addition to the above compensation. No wonder Haughey's gifts to Labour had topped £1 million. We were paying.

Lanarkshire Labour Mafia
Jenny Geddes

Was John Reid smoking something when he claimed the 85 pence worth of cannabis found in his house was not connected to him? Course it was mate. It was in your house. OK, you may have not been partaking or even know who was partaking but it got in there somehow.

Considering the company Dr Reid and Lanarkshire Labour keeps, maybe the police should be furthering their inquiries. In October 2002 the Lanarkshire Labour party held a Red Rose Fundraising Dinner. One of the guests was a notorious drug baron called Justin McAlroy. In September 2005 John Reid's son married the daughter of Ronnie Campbell – a west of Scotland gangland figure. Heaven knows how Labour gets away with having such links but don't expect Strathclyde Police to do a Met and start taking the law more seriously.

Maybe they were policing some of the interminable marches by certain Irish organisations that blight the area or investigating the links between Ulster paramilitaries and organised crime.

Sectarianism in the Labour Party was something the former Labour First Minister Henry McLeish complained about in March 2002 when he said that he had been marked out because he wasn't Protestant, Catholic, hadn't gone to Glasgow University and wasn't part of the Lanarkshire Labour mafia.

In October 2002 First Minster Jack McConnell confirmed this sectarianism in Lanarkshire Labour when he admitted hearing some Labour members say, "You cannot vote for him, his wife is called Bridget," while others warned that McConnell should not be backed because he was "a Proddie".

Since then he went on a public crusade against Scotland's "shame" by publicly lambasting myriad organisations for not doing enough. This resulted in criticism from one football chairman, the Orange Lodge saying it was being unfairly singled out, and the unprecedented remarks of the Catholic Church who said the issue was being overblown.

The response has seen some positive moves by both Rangers and Celtic Football Clubs and march organisers signing a joint declaration to behave. The Catholic Church even gave the Orange Order's Grand Master a column in the Scottish Catholic Observer – but more to spite McConnell than because of him.

However, one organisation has been strangely silent on how it would tackle the admitted sectarianism within its ranks. You've guessed it. The Labour Party.

The Scottish Dome
Jenny Geddes

I f we wrote the whole saga of the Holyrood project it would need a new book. But there are notable incidents pointing to Labour's sleazy attitude for letting an initial estimate balloon from £50 million to over £400 million.

In March 1998 the Spanish architect Enric Miralles was shortlisted for the Scottish Parliament contract. Nothing odd about that you would think. However, he had been rejected by the then project manager Bill Armstrong. Armstrong put him 44th out of 70 and if he'd known Miralles had no UK insurance cover he would have been number 70.

So who did shortlist him? The finger points at Scottish Secretary Donald Dewar for wanting a Catalan to dish the Nats. Armstrong eventually resigned over the political interference.

In January 1999 Bovis Lend Lease got the contract to build the Parliament. This was despite being initially eliminated from the tender process for being too expensive.

Since no Parliament had even been elected this mysterious reinstatement can only have been done by the Labour-run Scottish Office. Was it coincidence that McAlpine had been rejected despite having the lowest bid and because they had been donors to the Conservative Party?

Is it also coincidence that in May 2001 Robin Young, former non-executive director of Bovis, was appointed permanent secretary at the DTI? Weren't Bovis earning enough from an open-ended contract that made a mockery of the £50 million estimate?

By June 1999 there were fresh-faced MSPs ready to vote on handing control of the project to the Parliament from the Executive. It passed by three votes. It transpired later that extra costs on risk assessment were not disclosed by Executive Ministers during the debate. The then Finance Minister was one Jack McConnell – present First Minister.

Then we have a construction firm, O'Rourke Group, revealed in July 2002 as earning £36m for a Scottish Parliament building contract given by Bovis. The O'Rourke Group is a donor to the Labour Party.

But it still doesn't end there. In January 2005 Sarah Davidson, once adviser to former Scottish secretary Helen Liddell, landed £75,000 a year to enforce McConnell's smoking ban. The new job was never advertised.

What has this to do with Holyrood? She was the civil servant who presided over a £200m rise in the cost of Holyrood before taking a six-month sabbatical to travel round the world.

Mr Blunkett's Many Homes
Grant Morrison

When David Blunkett stood up to make his maiden speech in 1987 few can have guessed how literally he would take himself. He made clear he felt Government should support "… their tenants to ensure that together they are able to repair the desperate housing stock currently existing in many of our major areas". Mr Blunkett was obviously so keen to help that when he entered Government he took the first opportunity to subsidise the renovations to a rundown house in Wimbledon, owned by one "David Blunkett". Whilst Mr Blunkett lived in his grace-and-favour flat in Belgravia, he was receiving £700 a month in rent for his Wimbledon house, which he was using to renovate the property. Mr Blunkett felt it unnecessary to declare the extra income in the Register of Members' Interests although the rules stated that any "significant" income should be declared.

During his maiden speech Mr Blunkett also made his thoughts clear on property ownership, saying, "Talk of a property or share or capital owning democracy is an insult to the people of Sheffield Brightside." True to his word Mr Blunkett has done much over the years to avoid paying a mortgage. More than a year after his (second) resignation from the Cabinet Mr Blunkett was still living rent free in his £3million 'dis'-grace-and-favour flat in

Belgravia. Mr Blunkett felt it would be uncivilised for us to ask him to move out any faster.

Luckily, Mr Blunkett had somewhere quieter to muse over his long-awaited move from Belgravia. On the Chatsworth estate is his taxpayer-subsidised cottage that we must assume is essential to his job as a backbench MP. Perhaps the 15-mile journey from Chatsworth to Mr Blunkett's Sheffield Brightside home is further than an old socialist can be expected to travel after a hard day relaxing on one of the country's grandest estates at the taxpayers' expense.

However, it's nice to know that despite his long and highly subsidised journey up the property ladder Mr Blunkett still hasn't forgotten the people of Sheffield Brightside. Whilst writing to voice concerns over a proposed development near his Sheffield house there was an unfortunate mix-up and rather than being written on standard notepaper his objections were written and sent on much 'weightier' official notepaper – well, after all, one day he might want to visit there again and who knows maybe even stay the night.

But as they say, "Every cloud has a silver lining", and as we sit here and stare into the black hole that is the Government finances and wonder how we'll afford our own retirements we, the great British public, have at least one thing to be grateful for. Mr Blunkett won't be making another maiden speech.

Luvved up – Gordon on Film
Damon Lambert

Despite his macho and unnecessary workaholism, many will be surprised to know that official portraits state that the Chancellor has interests, and one of them is film. Wilf Stevenson, one of his university mates was a long-term director of the British Film Institute. Indeed, the first party Gordon Brown held at Number 11 was for movie-makers. Handed out to those long time Labour-loving luvvies with the cheese straws was the Bucks fizz of taxpayers' cash, in the form of tax reliefs. The Cassandras at the Treasury had predicted the reliefs would be used to avoid tax, just like the loopholes Brown spent the pre-1997 years lecturing the public that Labour would close. And don't forget this was in addition to Lottery and licence fee monies.

The cost of these tax incentives was estimated to be £15 million. Due to the predicted avoidance, it turned out to be £540 million per year, or about 0.5p off the tax rate for all corporates. This 'boost' to UK Film has not worked. The number of British films fell from 80 in 1997 to less than 40 in 2005 and British film exports actually dropped. A number of co-produced films have arisen to take benefit of these schemes. In 2005 there were 91 of these, only 15 of which were UK-produced. The logical thing would therefore be to abolish the reliefs. Usually New Labour never loses a chance to slam UK business for what Brown paints as tax avoidance. No chance. In 2005, in the week prior to the dissolution of Parliament just before the general election, the Government insisted on extending the reliefs, ramming the clauses through Parliament in an incredibly short Finance Bill debate that had not a single contribution from a Labour back-bencher. Still, it kept a film industry, not desperately fond of Iraq wars, content. Whilst incompetence can never be ruled out when Red Dawn Primarolo is in the mix, this has all the hallmarks of government that lectures everyone else on the morality of paying tax, permitting avoidance as long as it benefits its artistic chums.

Taxcutter, http://thetaxcutter.blogspot.com

Kinnock and the EU Whistle-blowers
Michael Wood

How could we write a book on fraud and corruption without mentioning the European Union? Whether it's agricultural payments for olive fields larger than the region that they're supposed to be in, or structural funds for motorways that stop in the middle of nowhere, you might think that there's little that even Labour politicians could teach Brussels about sleaze. You might think that, but you should know better.

Every now and again, even the EU realises that things have gone too far – that it's time that something was done to clean up the act. When those times come, you can rely on Labour to defend the status quo.

In December 1998 – back when Tony Blair was still a "pretty straight sort of guy" and Peter Mandelson was resigning for the first time – Paul van Buitenen, an assistant auditor in the European Commission, blew the whistle on widespread financial irregularities and mismanagement within the Commission. For this service, he was suspended on half pay pending disciplinary action.

Labour's reaction was swift. The leader of the Socialist MEPs, Pauline Green, supported all the Commissioners named in Mr van Buitenen's report and opposed motions calling for them to resign. The photos of Neil Kinnock thanking Mrs Green, after Labour votes ensured a majority in favour of the Commissioners staying in post, were soon seen around Europe.

Of course Labour's efforts to protect the corrupt Commissioners could only be successful for so long. In March 1999, the Commission became the first in history to be forced to resign and so a new Commission was nominated.

As if to prove that EU politicians do have a sense of humour, the new Commission President announced that the man he was putting in charge of stamping out sleaze was Neil Kinnock. Kinnock – one of the four 'resigning' Commissioners who kept their jobs – was not implicated in van Buitenen's allegations. However, any hope that anyone might have had that he would tackle EU fraud was soon to be proven misplaced.

One of the areas that Mr van Buitenen had identified as being riddled with fraud and nepotism was Eurostat – the Commission's statistical office – but it soon became clear that van Buitenen's allegations were only the tip of the iceberg. In January 2001, Dorte Schmidt Brown, a head of unit in Eurostat, wrote to Neil Kinnock with concerns about suspicious contracts worth millions. Unfortunately for Mrs Schmidt Brown, Commissioner Kinnock's response was inaction – leaving her victim to a campaign of threats and harassment, resulting in a nervous breakdown. Later, Mr Kinnock was forced to publicly apologise to her. Like other EU whistle-blowers who came forward, Mrs Schmidt Brown's career was over.

On the other hand, inaction would probably have been

better than the "reward" that Marta Andreasen, the first qualified accountant to be employed as the Commission's chief accountant, received when she complained about the EU's "Enron-style bookkeeping". Initially suspended by Neil Kinnock and barred from all Commission buildings, she has now been sacked without pay – even though internal Commission documents have largely supported her claims.

Jules Muis, the Commission's senior auditor, had written to his boss – Neil Kinnock – warning him that Mrs Andreasen's claims were "factually and substantively correct". He has since resigned, complaining that the Commission prevented him from investigating fraud and that they took "no responsibility for whether the accounts are right in the end".

If only as much energy was put into investigating corruption as was put into victimising those brave enough to uncover it.

Transforming Government
Jonathan Sheppard

If there is one area of life where Labour has done most damage it is the overt politicisation of all aspects of everyday life. As a schoolboy you were taught that the Civil Service, as with other key jobs, should be impartial and neutral. Under New Labour there has been an onslaught of political appointments in an effort to ensure that anything New Labour wants, New Labour gets.

This politicisation was most apparent during the recent vote on terror detention plans. Police forces became embroiled in politics with Chiefs of Police actively lobbying politicians in favour of a limit of 90 days for detaining terror suspects. Given that every Chief Constable was well aware that their job would be up for re-election, can it be right for our Chiefs of Police to be involved in lobbying for Government policy? How can their position be then tenable if there is a change of Government and a change in policy? It can't be, and that is why these kinds of position have to maintain their political neutrality.

From political appointments to non-elected quangos, to Chiefs of Police lobbying on behalf of Government policy, right through to an unprecedented increase in the number of Special Advisors at the heart of Government who have a remit no one could have imagined a few years previously, New Labour has indeed transformed Government, but, unfortunately, for the worse.

Fooling Some of the People
Chris Palmer

When you're stuck for something new to announce, why not re-announce something you've already released and pretend it's something new? No one will notice – and while you're at it, fiddle the facts just for added effect. This is the maxim which the Chancellor of the Exchequer and successive New Labour Education and Health Secretaries have lived by for the past nine years.

This Labour Government treats the electorate and its own voters with complete contempt, believing them all to be gullible, stupid fools.

Famously, between 1998 and 2000, David Blunkett (then Education Secretary) announced every year that the Education budget would increase by an "extra £19 billion", where in actual fact, this £19 billion was really far, far less. However, not content with the magical conversion of £9.7 billion into £19 billion. How so, you ask? Nick Davies of the *Guardian* explains: "So where is the £19 billion? Maybe it is already in the schools and we have simply failed to observe it. Maybe it is on its way down the pipeline and will arrive any week now. Or maybe it never existed. Maybe the truth is that Mr Blunkett's £19bn is largely composed of magical money, literally billions of pounds which have been conjured out of thin air by trickery – double-counting, treble-counting, several bookkeeping manoeuvres and a steady stream of fundamentally misleading public statements. Watch closely and you can see the conjuror at work. The first trick is the biggest."

Ever since the birth of inflation, government departmentments have been increasing their spending each year. When Mr Blunkett made his grand announcement in July 1998, he was reporting the results for education of Gordon Brown's comprehensive spending review, which had laid down a budget for every Whitehall department for each of the final three years of the parliament. The existing budget for UK education, for 1998/9, was £38.3 billion. As a result of the review, Mr Blunkett was able to announce that this would rise, in 1999, by £3 billion; in 2000, by £3.5 billion; and finally, in 2001/2, by £3.2 billion. That was all he announced. But, of course that adds up to only £9.7 billion. Where was the rest of the £19 billion? The answer is that it does not exist. Contrary to Mr Blunkett's description of his £19 billion as "real", nearly half of it is manufactured by a single bookkeeping trick. It works like this. You take the increase for the first year and you say, "Well, if I pay this in the first year, it will become a permanent part of the budget, so I will still be paying it in subsequent years when I make further annual increases, so I should carry on counting it as an increase each year." This is not the way that any British government has previously accounted for its budgets. Carl Emmerson of the Institute for Fiscal Studies says it is "misleading"; David Heald, professor of accountancy at

Aberdeen university and adviser to the treasury select committee, says it is "confusing" and "unprecedented". But, for Mr Blunkett, the result was simply excellent. In year one, he had a rise of £3 billion. In year two, he had a rise of £3.5 billion but he added in the £3 billion which he would still be paying from year one and called it a rise of £6.5 billion. Then he came to year three, when he had a rise of £3.2 billion, but he added in the £6.5 billion which he had already committed to the budget in the first two years and called it a rise of £9.7 billion. Then he stood back and added the whole lot up – £3 billion plus £6.5 billion plus £9.7 billion. A £19.2 billion bonanza.

Clear? Mr Blunkett and his ministers continued to indulge repeatedly in another kind of press trickery. They recycled money through a sequence of different announcements, each time pretending that they were unveiling brand new spending when, in truth, they were simply delivering old money in new clothes.

David Blunkett later moved on to become Home Secretary where he continued to concoct schemes with the same old set of tricks, with multiple releases to the press on the same topic, that attempted to portray Home Office inaction as progress. However, we all know now, that due to his deception and gross incompetence, much of the blame over the 1,000 foreign prisoners debacle can be placed at his door.

www.chrispalmer.org

Psychological Flaws
Paul Linford

"Your enemies are the people who sit behind you. Those in front are merely your opponents." Never was the old saying about the nature of politics more true than in the case of New Labour.

Under Tony Blair and his spin twins Peter Mandelson and Alastair Campbell, the practice of smearing one's own side was developed into a fine art.

The earliest victim was Dr David Clark. Appointed public services minister in 1997, stories soon appeared that he was spending a fortune jetting round the world looking at other countries' freedom of information legislation.

Then, in October 1997, the political editor of Clark's local paper, the *Newcastle Journal*, was startled to hear a Downing Street spin doctor tell him down the phone that Clark had "lost it" and would be sacked in the next reshuffle.

The aim of all this was twofold. First, Clark had to be got rid of because he had made the mistake of assuming Labour intended to act on its pre-election promise to bring in a wide-ranging freedom of information act, as opposed to the damp squib that finally emerged.

Second, as Paddy Ashdown's memoirs later made clear, Blair was at this time attempting to create two Cabinet vacancies to enable him to bring in Liberal Democrats, and Clark was one of those deemed dispensable.

In the event Clark survived another nine months, but he was not the only North-East MP who found himself on the wrong end of Blair's spin machine.

A couple of years later, the late Mo Mowlam, who had embarrassed Blair by earning a standing ovation during his conference speech, decided to quit politics after unnamed Labour sources openly questioned her sanity.

The most famous internecine New Labour smear of all, though, came in an interview with the *Observer*'s Andrew Rawnsley in 1998.

Rawnsley reported that someone "with an extremely good claim to know the mind of the Prime Minister" had described the Chancellor to him as "psychologically flawed".

Quite properly, Rawnsley has always refused to reveal his source, but Messrs Campbell and Mandelson head a shortlist of two.

With friends like those, New Labour has never been in need of enemies.

www.paullinford.blogspot.com

Blairways Holidays – Even Cheaper Than Chips...

Steve Garrett

Over the entire period of Blair's premiership, through that crisis, this reshuffle, those international tensions, that tsunami and the war, one activity has remained solidly unaffected within the Blair household. Nothing but nothing can shift the resolve of 'Team Blair' to get away from it all and have a really good time – preferably at someone else's expense. It is of course, the annual Blair holiday (or in the case of Team Blair, annual holidays – plural). Tone, Cherie, the kids and invited friends have made it their number one family priority to have a few months away every year – the more exotic, the better. Their number two priority seems to be to try to get someone else to pick up the tab.

They appear to have been entirely successful in both aims.

Crinkly warbler Sir Cliff Richard and former Italian PM Silvio Berlusconi have more than healthy Mediterranean tans, a mouthful of capped teeth and creative hairstyles in common. They both own rather nice exotic holiday homes in sexy locations. Add the odd minor European nobleman with the essential chateau or Tuscan villa, some big-shot city moneyman's exotic condo and you have Team Blair's very own, very private, very exclusive holiday brochure from which they choose. Hmmm, that's handy.

Not for Tony and Cherie the bother of searching the internet for bargain basement holiday deals. Not for them the hassle of queuing, pushing and shoving through passport control, waiting for luggage still somewhere over the Atlantic, arguing with a jobsworth in a peak cap and wondering whether the Latin taxi driver's car actually has any brakes under the bonnet.... Why? Because they have enlisted the help of the Queen's Flight to ease their way to their exclusive holiday destination. Hmmm, how sweet.

So, in short, it's win-win for the Blairs on their world tour. They fly for free, we pick up the tab. They stay for free, courtesy of one long line of apparently willing millionaires and their holiday homes.

When it comes to 'front', Team Blair seem to know no boundaries. When challenged about the apparent readiness to accept free holidays and utilise the Queen's Flight to get them there, Tony Blair always makes a point of giving a donation to some charity or other. He sees it as a sort of supposedly noble justification for all the special treatment and holiday favours he calls in. How much is donated – Blair presumably has set the figure, but how does he work it out? Is a tenner enough, or would a monkey or even a pony suffice? Hmmm, Gordon, lend us your calculator will you?

A month or two ago, after much pushing, Downing Street was forced to publish the actual real cost to the taxpayer of a Team Blair holiday trip to Sharm el Sheikh in Egypt. The amount came to well over £25,000 to the taxpayer... Did Tony's charitable donation dig that deep in his pocket? I doubt it. What a truly wondrous system Team Blair have invented for themselves. They blag a freebie holiday, they get the Queen's Flight to drop them off and pick them up, then Blair decides how much he should donate in lieu! Hmmm, how convenient.

Would it work for us? Could we get the Queen's Flight to drop us off in our holiday destination in Spain? Could we blag a few weeks at some plutocrat's Caribbean pad?

Talking of Cliff, this curious piece appeared on Popbitch in April 2006: "Friends of Sir Cliff Richard are claiming that Sir Cliff was far from happy with Tony and Cherie borrowing his house in Barbados. The first time he lent them his home, the singer was apparently disappointed that they didn't offer anything. When the Blairs asked again, Sir Cliff grudgingly said yes, but insisted on an arrangement where the PM would make an appropriate donation to Cliff's favourite charity. Some months later, the charity's accountants were asked about the payment. They confirmed a donation had been made as requested. But how much did the Blairs decide to pay? Cliff's friends are putting it about that the amount the PM thought was appropriate to rent a luxury villa in Barbados for over two weeks... was about the cost of a meal for two in a London restaurant."

So, they paid about £200 quid for a three-week holiday. Obviously Cherie was writing the cheque.

I know Blair has been cleared of improper conduct regarding his holiday arrangements – but that still doesn't stop me thinking that these very rich and very well connected celebs, foreign politicians and mega-rich moneymen hosts would perhaps expect a favour or two in return for their hospitality?

'Back scratching' is, after all, an entirely human condition.

Perhaps the Blairs should take a leaf out of a previous Labour Prime Minister's more modest and less controversial holiday arrangements. I've heard the Scilly Islands just off the coast of Cornwall are very nice at this time of year...

Wakin Hereward http://wakinghereward.blogspot.com

Spin Doctors Double Under Labour
Phil Taylor

Pretty much as soon as New Labour got into power it started undermining the impartiality of the Civil Service and diverting government funds to special advisers who were essentially Labour stooges paid by the State.

As early as October 2001 John Prescott gave the following answer in Parliament: "I can confirm that there are 81 special advisers... Indeed, I can confirm that the number of special advisers has increased from 38 – the number in post when we first came to office."

By July 2003 Downing Street had to admit that taxpayers had spent £5.4 million on special advisers in the 2002-03 tax year, more than double the amount spent in Labour's first year in power.

In February 2004 Tony Blair was criticised by the outgoing Commissioner on Standards in Public Life for failing to curb the power of these unelected special advisers. Sir Nigel Wicks was reported to have said that Mr Blair's reluctance to limit the influence of politically appointed spin doctors could further erode the public's trust in government.

The Government refused to accept the committee's proposal that special advisers should be defined as a category of government servant distinct from the Civil Service; that Parliament should set a limit on their number; and that Parliament should approve the granting of executive powers to people like Blair's chief of staff, Jonathan Powell, and his director of communications David Hill, who succeeded Alastair Campbell.

One of the scandals of the whole special advisor system is that they are allowed to bunk off at election time and work for their political masters at taxpayers' expense.

Special advisers are basically temporary civil servants who are exempt from the normal rules of civil service impartiality. Most are Labour activists. Under the terms of their contract, advisers who resign at election time are entitled to three months to six months' pay. Subsequently, if they are reappointed after the election they can pick up where they left off, having been paid by the state without interruption. Their "volunteering" is paid for by the state.

In the run-up to the last general election Andrew Tyrie, a Tory Treasury spokesman, said, "When the election is called, hordes of Labour advisers, most of whom have been doing nothing for months except work for the re-election of Labour, are going to descend on Labour HQ. The numbers are now so large that there is a de facto Labour Party campaign team working within Whitehall at the taxpayers' expense."

Nice work if you can get it.